Centerville Library
Washington-Cente~~DISCARD~~brary
Centerville, Ohio

PRAISE FOR

How to Succeed with Your Homeowners Association

"This book applies a common-sense approach to living in an HOA."

—Warren Davidoff, Ross Morgan and Company

"Linda Perret . . . the fact is she is a godsend for our community. While chairing meetings as a director, I frequently turned to her for guidance to contain the passionate energies of homeowners who simply want the best for their community. Her book offers down-to-earth, pragmatic information on the business of HOAs for the homeowners, volunteer directors, committee members, and hired management companies. These entities must collaborate to form a functional, pleasant community to live in as well as to protect and maintain the value of the property. Sounds easy, but not without Linda's guidance. If you have anything to do with an HOA, this is a must read, and keep this as a reference book! I didn't want to share Linda, but now we all have her vast knowledge and experience at our fingertips with *How to Succeed with Your Homeowners Association*."

—Laura Melton, board member

"I've worked with Linda for many years. She understands the process of HOAs and explains it in a way that's easy to understand."

—Mike Marsh, manager, Gold Coast Management

D1433017

Centerville Library
Washington-Centerville Public Library
Centerville, Ohio

HOW TO
Succeed
WITH YOUR
Home
Owners
Association

Copyright © 2016 by Linda Perret

All rights reserved.

Published by Familius LLC, www.familius.com

Familius books are available at special discounts for bulk purchases, whether for sales promotions or for family or corporate use. For more information, contact Familius Sales at 559-876-2170 or email orders@familius.com.

Reproduction of this book in any manner, in whole or in part, without written permission of the publisher is prohibited.

Library of Congress Cataloging-in-Publication Data

2015955939

Print ISBN 9781942934486

Ebook ISBN 9781944822132

Hardcover ISBN 9781944822149

Printed in the United States of America

Edited by Stephanie Yan

Cover design by David Miles

Book design by Lindsay Painter Sandberg

10 9 8 7 6 5 4 3 2 1

First Edition

HOW TO

Succeed

WITH YOUR

Home
Owners
Association

To my mom and dad, who encouraged me to write this book and who listened to all my HOA stories.

CONTENTS

Introduction

For many of us, one of the happiest days of our lives is when we buy our home. It may be our first home, a bigger dwelling for our family, maybe even our dream house—in some cases, all of the above. It might be a single-family home, townhouse, duplex, or condominium. For sixty-two million people, this new purchase comes with not only a mortgage but also a homeowners association.

It may be called an HOA (Homeowners Association), a PUD (Planned Urban Development), a Condo, a Maintenance Corporation, a Co-Op, or a Common Interest Development. No matter what you call it, the basic idea is the same—a group of homes, attached or unattached, that is governed by the same regulations and authorities. Just like your city has a local government that is run by a council, your HOA is a small government that is run by a board of directors.

Most people are aware that they are buying into an association when they buy a house, but many have no idea what that entails. What can make it even more difficult is that each HOA is unique. Each one has its own rules, enforcement, and protocol. This can make it confusing for a new homeowner.

During the close of escrow, the details of your HOA are disclosed to you in the governing documents, which include the Covenants, Conditions, and Restrictions (more commonly called "CC&Rs"); the Bylaws; and the Rules and Regulations. Of course, these documents, which can be hundreds of pages, come to you with a slew of other paperwork that you need to work through before getting the keys to your home. Few people take the time to actually read and understand these pages. It's not until after they've moved in and unpacked that they find out what restrictions are governing them.

Not reading the paperwork sometimes means that their first interaction with the HOA comes in the form of a violation notice from the association to "cease and desist" some behavior or action. It's not the nicest welcome to a community.

I know one homeowner who began tiling his living room within weeks of moving into a condominium. The HOA became aware of the unapproved work and immediately sent a letter explaining that it wasn't permitted and that he needed to restore the flooring to its original condition. The owner wasn't happy. He obviously was upset at the wasted expense and wanted to know how he was supposed to know about this restriction. I asked if he had received the CC&Rs, and he said, "Yes, I meant to read them but didn't have time."

His disregard for the rules wasn't intentional, and he corrected the situation as soon as he was made aware of it. But the situation could have been avoided if he had read the CC&Rs before starting the work. Incidents like this can leave a bad taste in a homeowner's mouth and lead to friction between the homeowner, the neighbors, and the association. This is one reason why HOAs have a less-than-stellar reputation. But that reputation isn't always deserved.

I've worked with HOAs for close to twenty years and attended over five thousand HOA board meetings as a recording secretary. (My own personal record was four meetings in one day. It was a very long day.) In that capacity, it's my responsibility to attend board meetings and draft the minutes. I get to hear all the dirt without having to get my hands dirty.

During my tenure, I've worked with management companies, been a property manager, assisted managers, and been hired directly by HOAs as a consultant to deal with homeowner issues. My job description grew to include site inspections and managing correspondence. I've experienced HOAs from almost every angle. There have been arguments, disagreements, name-calling, and legal fights. I've seen and experienced the frustrations associated with working with a board, management, and other homeowners.

But I've seen the good side of HOAs, too. Following the 1994 Northridge earthquake in southern California, I saw communities pull together and accomplish some amazing things. There are HOAs that collect food and toys for charity every holiday season. One community even rallied around two young girls who were left orphaned by a horrific car accident. The neighborhood raised enough money so the girls and their grandparents didn't have to move out of the family's home. I've witnessed people in associations work hard for the betterment of their community.

When it comes to HOAs, I've learned to never say I've seen it all, because every time I think that, I'm proven wrong. But one thing I do know for sure is that living in an HOA doesn't have to be full of turmoil. You can live peacefully with your neighbors and work productively with your board. In these pages, we are going to look at how you, as a homeowner, can accomplish those goals.

In dealing with an HOA, there are two key components needed—education and communication. This applies whether you are a board member, a homeowner, or a manager. If either one is missing, that's usually when you have havoc, frustration, and discord. That's when the working relationship starts to break down, and it's hard to get anything accomplished.

Associations are aware that it's not easy for homeowners to know all the rules. One local condo building has an architectural feature throughout its complex of stucco ledges and stairs that just begs for a pot or decorative item to be placed on it. In fact, these ledges are called "pot shelves." The ironic part is that homeowners are banned from putting pots on their pot shelves. Homeowners become angry when they get cited for this violation because they feel the complaint is nitpicking. A comment I often hear is, "Don't you have anything better to do than go after me for a potted plant?"

The comment doesn't upset me; that's where the education part comes into play. The association has the responsibility of educating homeowners on not only the rules but the reasoning behind them. I simply explain that this is a requirement by the association's insurance. The insurer decided they didn't want anything on the shelves that could fall, be knocked down, or get blown onto the stairs, as the stairs are the only way to get to and from each unit. If the association didn't enforce the restriction, its insurance could be canceled, so the rule was adopted and enforced.

Once the homeowner is *educated* on the rule and the logic *communicated*, the problem is usually resolved. Homeowners are more inclined to abide by a rule when they know the reasoning behind it. They may not like it, but they will respect it.

In this book, we'll show how communication and education on your part, the association's, and the management's can work together to create a fine-running machine. Although I may touch on some of the legalities involved in community living, that's not the focus. Instead, we're going to look at how you can apply common-sense approaches to understanding and succeeding with your HOA.

It's important to note that all of my experience has taken place in the state of California. HOAs can be found in all fifty states, but each state is different in how it governs. Some states, like California and Florida, are very strict and have many ordinances; others are a little more loosey-goosey. Some of the examples I use may apply only to California, as that's the state I'm familiar with. Your state may have different codes, but even if the specifics don't apply to you, you should be able to use the principles behind the example.

Another point that needs to be stressed is that these words are meant to educate homeowners. They are not intended, nor should they be perceived, as legal advice.

No matter what your present situation is, this book can help you succeed with your HOA. If you are a new homeowner just getting ready to purchase your first home in a community, don't fret. HOAs are manageable. This book will help take away some of the fears and confusion you may be facing.

If you are a homeowner who is living in an HOA and things aren't going as smoothly as you hoped, don't despair. Your home and your family are worth protecting, and you can take steps to change your current situation. HOAs are always evolving, and although you may be dealing with issues now, know that it's not permanent.

If you live in an HOA now and things are going well . . . enjoy! It's a wonderful feeling when everyone is getting along, so just soak it up and relish in it.

INTRODUCTION
TO AN HOA

What Is an HOA?

You find your dream house, secure a mortgage, go through the rigmarole of escrow, pack up the boxes, put them in the van, and move into your new home. During the process, you were made aware your new home was in an "association," but what is a homeowners association? And more importantly—what does that really mean to you?

An HOA is an organization that owns and/or governs property in a community. That community can consist of single-family homes, condominiums, mobile homes, or any other type of dwelling. That's the simple definition, but as with most things in life, there's a lot more to it. And that's true when dealing with an HOA.

When you buy into an association, you become not only the owner of your individual property but also a part owner of the association. If there are 200 homes in your association, then you are 1/200 of an owner of the association's property. This means you have an interest or stake in all the common areas owned by your association and share in the liabilities for these elements.

Common areas can include amenities such as community pools, clubhouses, parks, guardhouses, streets, landscaping, and, in some cases, even a home or two. They can range from minimal to quite extensive. Gated communities tend to have more common areas because once an area is enclosed with a gate and restricts access to the general public, the HOA takes over ownership and responsibility for everything contained within those gates. A gated community may have the added expenses of sewers, street lights, traffic signs, and signals. The HOA is responsible for the maintenance of all its common components, and as a member of the association, you share in that task.

I currently work for one HOA that is dealing with a lot of traffic issues. At almost every meeting, a homeowner asks the board to gate the community so they can keep the speeders off their streets. Every month, the board reiterates that undertaking this burden would be expensive and most likely result in a stiff increase in the monthly assessments. The homeowner responds with, "No, I called a fence company, and it will only cost about $35,000 to install a fence." The homeowner has good intentions, but she didn't take into account such items as maintenance of the gate; repairs; responsibility for the sidewalks, curbs, lights, traffic-calming devices, and that once streets are enclosed by a fence and gate, they become the association's property; along with the legalities of petitioning the City to allow the takeover of the streets. Many of these costs are long term and would continue to be a burden on the community.

In addition to overseeing the common areas, the HOA holds each member accountable. It makes sure that you and your neighbors are keeping up your individual properties, that the rules are being followed, and that assessments are being paid. These are what help to maintain and even increase your property values.

What gives the HOA the right to do all these things on your behalf? The deed to your property. Incorporated into that little piece of paper is the condition that binds you to your HOA. It's similar to having a mortgage: if the bank is listed on the deed, you are indebted to that bank. If you don't pay your mortgage, they can take your house. You gave them that right. In fact, it was one of the conditions for them to loan you the money.

The same is true with your HOA. When you sign the deed to the property or house, you agree to and accept the terms and conditions of your particular HOA. When I started as a recording secretary, the monthly assessments were called "dues." You paid your monthly "dues." There was going to be an increase in the "dues." "Dues" was the common term. Then the big real estate slide hit and many people were losing money on their homes. They were upside down on their mortgages, meaning they owed more on the property than its actual value. Paying their monthly dues became a burden, and HOAs began to foreclose. There was a push back where people were saying, "How can you take my property for not paying 'dues'? I didn't pay the dues at my health club, and all they did was cancel me." Apparently the term "dues" was misleading, as it implied that membership in the HOA was optional, so HOAs went back to using the formalized term of "assessment."

But unlike an HOA, the bank goes away once you pay off the note. That doesn't happen with your association. Your HOA is here to stay. You are stuck with it until you either sell the house or, for some strange and very rare circumstance, the HOA dissolves. Don't get your hopes up on this, though. In twenty years of dealing with hundreds of homeowners associations, I've never seen one dissolve. It's a pretty good bet that if you buy a property that's part of an association, you will have to find a way to accept both the good and the bad of your HOA.

Membership in an HOA is generally not optional. There are a few cases, usually where the HOA was formed after the property's development, where you can decide if you want to belong or not. Being a member is completely voluntary. This type of association is more of a social club, and the HOA doesn't really have much power.

So if you currently have an HOA, get used to it, because it's probably going to be there for a while. There is good news—many of the horror stories you hear are exaggerated. It is possible to live harmoniously in an HOA.

What Are the Benefits of an HOA?

Some people consider "HOA benefits" an oxymoron. They feel there isn't a bright side to living in a planned community. But that really isn't true. In reality, HOAs provide a wide range of services for homeowners. Let's take a look at some of the benefits.

Common Area Amenities

An association can give you access to amenities that you otherwise wouldn't have or couldn't afford. These can include such things as a park, clubhouse, pool, sports court, or golf course, to name a few.

A pool is a luxury that many of us would like, but it comes with a pretty hefty price tag. You not only have the cost of building it in the first place, but you also have the monthly maintenance, upkeep, and repairs. These items can start to add up. But if your HOA has a community pool, these expenses are shared among all the members. Instead of paying 100% of these costs, you are only paying a portion of them. All of a sudden, a pool is affordable.

Another benefit is that all these amenities that you're buying into are going to be maintained by someone else. You pay your monthly dues, and the association takes care of the rest.

If you have a pool on your property, you need to take care of it. You can do this yourself, which can be time consuming, or you can hire a service, which can be inconvenient. And then, of course, the financial burden is all on you. If your association has a community pool, all of those issues transfer to the HOA. Management oversees the cleaning and upkeep of the pool. You pay for the service through your monthly assessments, and you get the luxury of spending your weekends sitting by the pool instead of cleaning it.

Overall Maintenance of the Community

One thing that attracts people to HOA living is the idea that someone else is going to do a lot of their everyday maintenance. This is especially true in condominium complexes and townhomes. The HOA is responsible for its property, which could include your front lawn, trees, streets, roofs, paint, and fencing. In some instances, you don't have to worry about when it's time to paint the exterior of your home because the association does that for you.

If a part of your home is in need of repair and it's a common area element, you're off the hook. It's the job of your association to get it fixed.

Handling Disputes between Neighbors

There's an old saying that "fences make good neighbors." This can be true, but there are other times when fences make for a good fight between neighbors.

It would be great if everyone living in a community got along with each other all the time, but it just doesn't happen. It doesn't mean there's something wrong with the community or with the people living there. Differences of opinions are a fact of life. We all have them, and occasionally the tensions escalate.

If such tensions erupt, your homeowners association can provide a buffer zone. Sometimes these disagreements stem from misinterpretation of the community rules on one or both sides. The association can make the final decision on these kinds of matters and set the rules that both sides must live by.

Even if the problem isn't that cut and dry, the association can be a mediator. In many cases, just having a third party present helps. The HOA can set up a neutral meeting place for the two sides to converge and discuss the issue. This can help resolve whatever the issue is and restore the peace without having to go the legal route.

Creating and Enforcing a Standard of Living

Imagine that you sink your life savings into your home. You love the neighborhood, and the quality of life is just as you imagine. Then a neighbor decides to open a mechanic's shop in his front yard. He has nonoperating vehicles in all stages of repair parked on the street, car parts stacked up in his front yard, and people coming and going at all hours of the day and night. You don't mind his entrepreneurial spirit, but you do resent the bite it is taking out of your property values—not to mention the noise and traffic that affects the quiet enjoyment of your home.

Dogs barking, loud parties, and inappropriate business activities can all cause turmoil and distress for the neighbors. Other issues may include improperly dumping trash, storing items on the property, and the overall condition of the house and appearance of the landscape. Your city may have ordinances that cover these issues, but so does your HOA.

When you purchase your home, you are also purchasing into a lifestyle. Your association should help you maintain that environment.

Maintaining Property Values

We've all experienced it: You spot a beautiful home. It's gorgeous, well landscaped, and simply picture perfect. You love it and are ready to move right in. But when you look next door, that house isn't so beautiful. It hasn't been painted, the lawn hasn't been mowed, and the cute picket fence has fallen down and been replaced with a chain-link fence. Three more houses down is another beautiful home that could grace the cover of *Homes and Gardens*, and next to that one is a home with the windows boarded up. This is what we call a "spotty" neighborhood. It's not very appealing to prospective buyers.

Or you look at another neighborhood where the houses are roughly the same size, except for one that is much bigger than the rest. Its walls extend from property line to property line. It may be a gorgeous home, but it looks out of place—something that is now being referred to as a McMansion. It can work the other way, too. You might be living in a community with large homes, then someone comes in and knocks his home down and builds two smaller ones. Or he turns the house into an apartment building.

In these cases, there is no consistency in the neighborhood. Unfortunately, this will affect the value of your home and your ability to resell it, no matter how nice you keep it. When you purchase your home, you want some insurance that the neighborhood and homes will remain the same. Your association can do this by enforcing building restrictions, remodel approval processes, and community rules. With these, you'll have some assurance that the community you bought into will remain the same.

This is likely the biggest and most important benefit of your HOA and the reason HOAs have become so popular. Your HOA maintains your property values. For an idea of how important property values are, just look at what happened to our economy right after the turn of the century when home values plummeted. People were underwater on their mortgages. Many homeowners found themselves in the position of owing more to the bank than what they could sell the property for. Homeowners stopped paying their mortgages and, along with that, were unable to pay their association dues. Foreclosures by either the bank or the HOA were rampant.

When you buy a property, you want its value to increase, or at the very least stay at the purchase-price level. You never want your property to go below the current market price, and an HOA can play a part in keeping property values consistent. Every association has mechanisms in place to remove nonpaying homeowners and to demand the upkeep of the property.

There are distinct advantages—increased amenities, a forum to handle disputes, enforcement of community standards, and maintaining property values—to living in an HOA. These positive aspects of planned communities come with their own sets of rules, regulations, and requirements, and that can be scary. But don't let the fear outweigh the potential benefits that you can glean from your HOA.

What Are the Disadvantages of an HOA?

We just talked about the positive side of living in an HOA, but I'm not naïve enough to think that it is all fun and games. Unfortunately, nothing is perfect in life, and that goes for your HOA, too. Here are some of the more common disadvantages:

Restrictions

One of the reasons many of us buy a home is that we want the freedom it affords us. We can paint the walls any color, hang pictures wherever, plant a garden, and do whatever we want—at least in theory. But a home you buy in an HOA comes with governing documents that may limit what you actually *can* do.

These restrictions are spelled out in the CC&Rs and the Rules and Regulations. Some of the limitations are extensive, while others are very minor. Either way, it is important you find out what rules are going to be governing you and your property **before** you purchase your home.

I bolded that "before" for good reason. One of the biggest sources of conflict between homeowners and the HOA is being unaware of or not understanding the rules that come into play after the close of escrow.

One homeowner found himself in that situation shortly after moving into a community that had a rule regarding portable basketball stands. These stands are heavy, huge, and although technically "portable," tough to move. In this community, they are allowed but only during play. If the kids aren't using them, they have to be moved to the backyard or put away completely—they can't be in view from the common area. This new homeowner was quickly cited for leaving his stand out. He came to the board and stated that the rule was unreasonable and "nobody in the community wanted the rule." He wasn't being difficult, but he truly felt it was a silly rule and nobody wanted it. The board explained that the rule was in existence when he moved in and the board had to enforce it. But it agreed to not impose any monetary fines temporarily in order to give the homeowner time to change the rule.

The board knew what the outcome would be. The homeowner petitioned others in the community and quickly found that he was in the minority. His neighbors did want the rule, and the homeowner ended up willingly removing his basketball stand. He wasn't fined because once he found out the rule wasn't going to change, he complied.

Luckily, this case was something minor and easily remedied. Some people purchase a new home only to find out they can't run their home business, keep their family dogs, or park their treasured RV in the community. Before signing on the dotted line, check the governing documents to make sure you can live with the restrictions. If you love pit bulls, want to raise chickens, or want to restore cars in your spare time, make sure these conditions are allowed prior to the purchase. The most frustrating situation for both homeowners and the association is when a new owner moves in, is aware of the existing rules, and just chooses to ignore them.

Another reason why you can't do whatever you want with your property is that in some cases, especially in condominiums and townhomes, the property is not yours. You are actually purchasing from the walls in—or, as it is sometimes called, "the air space." The exterior walls and outdoor property belongs to the association. In some cases, this can include the balcony or patio attached to your unit. This is what is called "exclusive use" area. You, as the owner of the unit, have the right to use it at the exclusion of all the other residents, but the property is actually owned by the association. Of course, the responsibility for maintaining it and keeping it clean usually comes along with your right to use it.

Cost

Another drawback to living in an association is the cost. You are required to pay a monthly assessment. Depending on the size of the association, number of homes in the association, property owned by the association, and amenities provided by the association, these monthly fees can range from a few extra dollars a month to thousands of dollars, with the norm being a couple hundred dollars.

To give you an idea of how assessments can vary, in my town, there is an HOA that owns no property. There are about one hundred single-family homes, and the utilities are all maintained by the city. So why do they have an HOA? They want to maintain the quality of the homes, and once a year, they throw a party for the community. Those are their only two expenses. To cover those costs, the fees to the homeowners are $10 a month. On the other hand, there is a neighboring HOA a few minutes away that has hundreds of homes, a clubhouse with a concierge, pool, gym, 24-hour guarded gate service, and dedicated patrol of the neighborhoods. Their monthly fee? $650 a month.

For many of us, money is a big concern when we are buying our first home and sometimes even when we are purchasing our second, third, or fourth. In order to prepare a household budget, you need to know what your monthly dues are. This information is given to you during escrow, and although HOAs are limited in how much they can increase the assessment, there are other unexpected costs that can creep up in the form of a special assessment. A special assessment is an additional assessment that can be imposed. They usually come about to deal with unexpected situations or unbudgeted expenditures. A board has the power to impose a special assessment of 5% or less of the annual operating budget without going to a vote of the membership. In an emergency, the board has the power to implement an unlimited special assessment to cover expenditures needed to correct a situation that poses an immediate threat to safety or damage to property. An emergency would be defined as an expense that the board couldn't have been able to anticipate when preparing the budget and would be detrimental to put off or one that is ordered by a court of law. Any other special assessments require a vote of the membership. In any case, this unknown can be a big negative.

Very rarely do monthly assessments decrease. It's more likely they will increase slightly each year. As a new homeowner, you should be prepared and budget for yearly increases.

Community Living

Living in an HOA also means living with the personalities that it encompasses. I maintain that you can get a feel for a community just by attending an HOA meeting. A board meeting is a good litmus test of the neighborhood. Are the homeowners courteous? Does the meeting start on time and run smoothly? Is the board respectful of the homeowners and vice versa? Is management prepared, organized, and knowledgeable? Is the meeting productive? But the most important question is probably: Are you comfortable with the people around you? The answers to these questions can give you an idea of what kind of community it is and what the people are like. After all, they are the ones who are going to be your neighbors.

If you are considering purchasing a home in a community with an HOA, here are a few things you can do before signing on the dotted line.

REQUEST AND READ THE MEETING MINUTES.

When you enter into escrow, you are entitled to copies of the minutes. Ask to receive the minutes from the past year. They may not give you that many, but it doesn't hurt to ask. Do make sure, though, that you get the most recent set of minutes. When you are purchasing, you want to see what you are buying into now.

Is there a mention of a special assessment? Are there any references to legal issues? Are topics carried over from one meeting to the next or do they tend to disappear? Are matters followed through to a conclusion? This is where having a year's worth of minutes can come in handy. They will give you a good idea of what is going on in the community and any issues that are being addressed.

ATTEND AN HOA MEETING *BEFORE* CLOSING ESCROW, IF PERMISSIBLE.

Not all associations will allow a prospective buyer to sit in on their meetings, but if they will allow it, take the opportunity to do so. It will give you great insight into the community you are buying into.

Most of us know about the importance of first impressions, and this principle applies to HOAs as well. I worked for one association where, after just one encounter with them, I knew that I would never live with these people even if they gave me a house in that tract. It started with a group of homeowners confronting me when I arrived, demanding to know what side I was on. I told them I was just there to do my job and didn't have a side. One guy responded, "We don't believe that." I knew him all of four seconds, and he was calling me a liar. I then went into the meeting room. I was early, as is a tendency with me, but when I walked in, I found the board in the midst of a meeting. I thought I was late, but the board president said, "No, we told you 6:30, but we like to meet at 5:00 so that we can make all of the decisions ahead of time." I was shocked and told them that wasn't allowed. The president quickly responded with, "It is if no one finds out about it." Oh dear.

During the course of the meeting, I discovered there weren't just two opposing sides but actually "groups" of homeowners feuding. (When I was asked which side I was on, I didn't know it was a multiple choice question.) Each group was suing the other and the board and the management. It was a mess. I stuck it out for a year before I politely resigned from the account. I couldn't imagine living in that chaotic environment that was evident at just one meeting.

Not too many of us would buy a house just from seeing a picture on the Internet. This same philosophy should also apply when buying into an HOA. Knowing what negatives may exist can help you be aware of what to look for during the purchasing process and keep you from being disappointed afterwards.

Despite these potential issues, not all HOAs are horror stories and buying into one doesn't have to be a bad experience. I have a number of accounts that I have worked with for years. The boards are professional, the homeowners are courteous, and they truly are what a community is supposed to be. People who live in these neighborhoods tend to stay for a long time, and it's easy to see why.

Even if you find yourself facing some of these negative situations, with a little work, you can turn your HOA into what you want and expect it to be.

What Makes Up an HOA?

We've talked about the good and the bad of living in an HOA, but there is more to it than simply knowing you have an HOA. When you sign on the dotted line, you not only are purchasing a house—you are becoming a part of an exclusive club: the association. The members are limited to those people who own a home in the neighborhood. In that sense, it is a private club, but it certainly isn't selective. The only requirement for joining is the ability to purchase property. This means you will have people with different lifestyles, different ideals, and different priorities all living together. When it works, it is beautiful. When it doesn't, it can be very turbulent.

In an attempt to reduce and minimize the disturbances, legislators (or the powers that be) have developed codes that we all must abide by. Every state has its own laws overseeing common interest developments. Some states, like California, where I live, have extensive codes, while others are more lenient. You want to check to see what laws your state has that apply to your community.

In an HOA, these laws or codes are what we call the "governing documents." Each individual HOA has its own set of governing documents. These are usually created by the developer before the first home is purchased. The governing documents consist of three elements: the Bylaws, the CC&Rs, and the Rules & Regulations.

Bylaws

Most HOAs are not-for-profit corporations, meaning they are businesses that are run by a board of directors. The board must operate within certain parameters which are found in the Bylaws. Basically, the Bylaws are the rules that your board must follow when acting on your behalf.

The Bylaws contain specifications on how many directors are allowed on the board, criteria for serving on a board, different officers or board positions to be filled, terms for board members, meeting requirements, and such.

The restrictions in the Bylaws don't usually affect homeowners on an individual level. They don't necessarily tell homeowners what they can and can't do with their personal property. But it is still important that you familiarize yourself with them. Your board of directors works for you, and you should know if it is following the rules.

A great example of this is a board that I worked with extensively. It had recently undergone some changes. They had all new faces on the board except for one, and this one was a doozy. He was making things unmanageable for the remaining board members. The other board members were thrilled when this man's home went on the market and sold quickly. As soon as escrow closed, they asked him to return the keys to the association's common areas, which were given to board members. They figured when he sold his unit, he also was giving up his seat on the board.

He refused. He said that he had no intention of resigning his seat on the board. A review of their Bylaws determined that there was no requirement that a board member had to actually be a member of the association, and therefore they couldn't get rid of him. He was able to continue making decisions for everyone else even though he didn't own a unit in the complex.

The above association could change this condition, as it is possible to revise or amend the Bylaws, but it usually takes a vote of the membership. The requirements to change the Bylaws are usually contained within the Bylaws.

CC&Rs

Now we are getting to the documents that affect your everyday life. CC&Rs stand for Covenants, Conditions, and Restrictions. Basically, these are the rules that apply to both your association and your home. They mandate not only what you can and can't do at your individual property but also the things that you *have* to do.

The actual form of the CC&Rs varies from property to property. You may have a book-like document with a table of contents or just a few pages stapled together. Some are well organized and easy to follow, while others are just one long paragraph. The CC&Rs for my home is simply a numbered list of things I can't do. But no matter how they are they presented, the CC&Rs will incorporate some of the following components.

The CC&Rs are created prior to the construction of a development. In order for a developer to sell a home in a planned community, the CC&Rs must be in place. That is why the first section of the CC&Rs usually covers the developer—or "declarant," as he or she is usually referred to in the CC&Rs. It's a lot of legal mumbo jumbo that basically says the developer doesn't have to follow the rules that are laid out for the homeowners.

Of course, I'm oversimplifying and being a little flippant because these rules really only apply while the developer is involved in the project. The CC&Rs are established by the developer before any units are completed and sold. In a lot of cases, they need to be in place prior to breaking ground. This section allows for the developer to continue construction and makes it easier to sell the homes, but it also makes it possible for individual homeowners to live in the community. Before building homes, the developer needs to submit a plan to the Department of Real Estate. This outlines how many homes are being built and the phases of construction. For example, if there are a hundred homes, there might be four phases. The developer will work on building twenty-five homes in the first phase. When these homes are completed, newcomers can move in and are bound by the rules found in the CC&Rs. The developer moves on to the next phase, homeowners begin moving in when it's complete, and so on until the project is built out and the developer leaves.

This portion of the CC&Rs will affect you only if you are buying into a new property that is still under the control of the developer. By the way, the Bylaws also have a section allowing the developer to be board members. Until a community reaches a certain percentage of ownership, the developer is the board and runs your association. As the units sell and ownership increases, the number of developer seats diminishes.

If you are buying into an established association, this section of the CC&Rs won't apply. In fact, some HOAs will revise their CC&Rs after the developer leaves to remove this language in its entirety.

With or without the involvement of the developer, the CC&Rs will spell out the responsibilities of the association. For a community of standalone homes, this is fairly simple. You are responsible for your property. The association is responsible for its property. When you buy into a townhome, a condo, or a shared property, this can get confusing. In a condo, you may not own the walls—so if a pipe breaks in the wall, then you aren't responsible, right? Not necessarily. Although you don't own it, the CC&Rs may mandate that you are required to maintain and repair pipes even if they are on association property.

The CC&Rs will also identify any known easements that the association has over the property. An easement is a legal document recorded over your property that gives the easement holder rights on your property. Most properties will have an easement over them held for the sake of utilities. In some cases, there are multiple and extensive easements. It's not unusual for your HOA to have some easements over your property. This may mean the HOA has the right to run irrigation lines through your parcel or that the association has the right to enter your property. It's important to note that sometimes the HOA has individual easements that apply to only one home. These are recorded separately and not part of the CC&Rs but should be made known to you during the escrow process.

It can be confusing trying to determine who is responsible for what. "Is the air conditioner a homeowner responsibility, or does my HOA cover that?" "If a window breaks, do I repair it?" "Do I clean my windows, or will my association?" In order to make this clearer—and to avoid potential litigation—some associations are developing a Responsibility Chart or Matrix. This is a spreadsheet developed, sometimes by legal counsel, that lists all the components of the HOA and units and whether the HOA or the homeowner is responsible for them. A Matrix might look something like this spreadsheet.

If your association doesn't have a Responsibility Matrix, you might want to suggest it to your board of directors, especially if you live in a condo where the lines of ownership are a little muddier. It can take some of the guesswork out of what you have to maintain and what you can expect from your HOA.

ABC HOMEOWNER'S ASSOCIATION RESPONSIBILITY MATRIX		
Maintenance Item	HO Responsibility	HOA Responsibility
Air Conditioning Unit	X	
Door - Front Door X		
Door Frame - Front Door		X
Garage Door		X
Garage Door Mechanism	X	
Garage Door Opener	X	
Exterior Hose Bib	X	
Mailbox - Key	X	
Mailbox Structure		X
Patios - Clean	X	
Patios - Maintenance		X
Pipes - Interior Walls*	X	X
Streets - Cleaning		X
Streets - Maintenance		X
Streets - Paving		X

In the CC&Rs, you will also find a section that you as a homeowner should pay particular attention to. This section will outline what you are responsible for and what you can and can't do. This may include where and what you can park in the community (some HOAs ban RVs; others don't allow parking in the streets) and how many and what kind of animals you can keep on your property. There generally is a clause that you must maintain your property in good condition. Some CC&Rs even dictate what color you can paint your house.

The CC&Rs are not suggestions or recommendations. These are the rules, and when you purchase your home, you should consider them written in stone. The CC&Rs are recorded over your property, meaning they are filed legally with the state or local government. In California, they are filed with the County Recorder's office. CC&Rs also convey, meaning they transfer with the property. The CC&Rs should be provided to you during escrow, and you should read them before closing the deal.

It is possible to change the CC&Rs, but it's not an easy process. Revision of the CC&Rs requires a vote of the community. Your Bylaws will determine the percentage needed to pass a revision. It may be a simple majority—50% + 1—or a super majority—75%. In some cases, and this is very rare, it is 100%. I've only seen the 100% requirement once, and that was a small condominium building that had only ten members. There are even some CC&Rs that require approval from the lenders. Getting 50% of any number of people to agree can be difficult. So when you are purchasing your home and there is a part of the CC&Rs that you can't live with, don't anticipate that it will be something that you can simply ignore or change easily.

Homeowners can't assume that revising the CC&R is a foregone conclusion. One man bought his first home in an association. He owned his own company and drove a large truck with his logo on the side. Shortly after moving in, he was cited by the HOA for parking the commercial truck in the driveway. The CC&Rs stated that no commercial vehicles could be parked in the community, even in the homeowner's own driveway. They further went on to stipulate that certain vehicles that were used solely for commercial ventures (i.e., limos, tow trucks, etc.) were barred from parking in the community. This man violated both rules and continued to park his vehicle in his driveway because it was too large to fit in the garage.

In defense of this man, he wasn't being ornery. He honestly didn't know this rule existed when he purchased the property and hadn't read the CC&Rs. He was parking the truck on his property and not the HOA's property. After racking up thousands of dollars in fines, he tried to amend the CC&Rs and quickly found out that he was in the minority. His neighbors didn't want trucks in the community, and the proposed amendment failed. He ended up selling his house and moving to a less restrictive community. But before he purchased his second home, he read the CC&Rs . . . thoroughly.

Rules and Regulations

By now, you may be thinking that all the dos and don'ts have been covered, but there is still one more list you have to deal with—the Rules and Regulations. Whereas the Bylaws and CC&Rs could apply generically to any development, the Rules and Regs, as they are called, are geared specifically toward your community.

Rules and Regs are developed by your board and implemented for the needs of your HOA's residents.

Unlike the Bylaws and the CC&Rs, the Rules and Regs are designed to be fluid and to change to reflect the needs of the community.

There is a process, though, for revising the Rules and Regs. Any proposed changes to the rules must be sent out to the membership for review. Homeowners must be given at least thirty days to review the proposed revisions prior to the board adopting them. During this time, the board must hold an open session meeting to allow members to voice their concerns or comments on the changes. Based upon the comments received, the board may alter the revision or it may proceed with the proposed changes. After the thirty-day review period, the board may adopt the revised rules. The adoption of the revised rules must take place in an open session meeting, and homeowners need to be notified within fifteen days of the board's formal resolution approving the amended rules. Once all this is done, the rules are in place and can be enforced.

Unlike the CC&Rs, the Rules and Regs don't require a vote of the membership. The board may ask for input from HOA members, but it is not bound to act on the homeowners' recommendations.

The Rules and Regs are designed to allow your HOA to enforce rules for the benefit of the residents. For example, your HOA may have a pool. It is an amenity that is included in your CC&Rs. But your rules may limit the use of this perk. For example, the pool can only be used between the hours of 8:00 a.m. and 10:00 p.m. This rule may work great for some time, but then some homeowners may petition the board to change the hours so they can swim before work. The board agrees and allows the pool to be open at 6:00 a.m.

After living in an HOA for a bit, you'll quickly find out that there are some rules you like and some you don't. Unfortunately, even if you don't like a rule, you still have to abide by it. But with some effort, rules can be changed.

If it's a rule that has been in effect for a period of time, then you will need to petition the board to make modifications. You can broach the subject during the open forum at a board meeting. Hopefully, if the board is receptive, it will take the initiative and begin the process to amend the rules.

If the board doesn't seem interested in taking any action, then your next step may be to get others involved.

Ask others in the community who are in agreement to attend the board meetings. If this isn't practical, then draft a petition and get signatures. If you get a majority of the homeowners to sign, chances are good the board will listen.

The procedure is a little easier for a rule that was just adopted. When a rule has been changed, the membership must be notified within fifteen days from when the revision was adopted. Within thirty days of the written notification, 5% of the membership can request a special meeting to reverse the rule change. The rule may then be reversed if there is a favorable majority of the votes at the duly held meeting in which a quorum is present.

So what does that mean? Let's say you live in an association with one hundred members. Your board passes a new rule banning pickup trucks in the community. You drive a Dodge Ram and think this is unfair. Many of your neighbors do too. So one week after you get the notice that the rule is now official, you get five of your fellow truck-loving neighbors to sign a petition to hold a Special Meeting to Reverse the Rule on Pickup Trucks. You deliver this to the association in accordance with your governing documents. The association is *required* to hold the meeting to address this concern, and the special meeting is scheduled. You need 51 households—not people—to establish a quorum. You get 64, either in person or through ballots/proxies, and you can proceed with your meeting. If the majority of the persons—33 households—vote to approve rescinding the rule, it is rescinded.

It is a lot of work to go through, but it is doable.

Architectural Guidelines

There is one last set of restrictions you may have to deal with, and that is the Architectural Guidelines. These are the rules that cover modifications and improvements that you can make to your property.

The Architectural Guidelines are similar to the Rules and Regs in the way they are amended and approved by the board. They go through the same procedure as the Rules and Regs. Items in the Architectural Guidelines are usually more specific than the CC&Rs and may spell out paint colors, structure height restrictions, approved plants, and use of outdoor space. It will usually include the process you need to follow for remodeling projects.

Not every HOA has Architectural Guidelines. Some HOAs cover these items in the CC&Rs and Rules and Regulations, but the Architectural Guidelines can be very limiting, so you want to be sure to review a copy if your HOA does have them.

The governing documents are specific to your individual community, but you are also held to local, state, and federal ordinances. As a nonprofit organization, an HOA is also bound by corporation codes.

In California, our HOAs adhere to the Davis-Stirling Common Interest Development Act—or, as it is more commonly called, Davis-Stirling. When residential common interest developments—or, as they are more commonly referred to today, HOAs—first started springing up in California, they were governed by corporation and civil codes. Many elements of these codes didn't apply to HOAs. There were other aspects of community living that civil and corporation codes didn't touch upon. So in 1985, a group of lawmakers, spearheaded by Lawrence Stirling and Gray Davis, compiled laws to govern associations. And soon their body of work became law and went into effect in 1986.

To get an idea of the popularity of HOAs, when the Davis-Stirling Act was first implemented, it was roughly twenty-five pages. Over the years, it has been tweaked, edited, and updated. In 2014, the Act was revised and had grown to over a hundred pages. Be sure to look into what codes—both state and local—affect your HOA.

It may seem like there are a lot of rules to living in an HOA—and unfortunately, there are—but there is a reason for it. And believe it or not, most people understand that. I was commiserating with a young clerk at a local retail establishment. She was telling me about all the problems she was having with her parents' HOA and not being able to park her car on the street. I said, "Sometimes the association's rules can be a pain." She thought about it and said, "Yeah, but without them, we wouldn't have such lovely communities." She is right.

PART ONE

THE

HOMEOWNERS

The Responsibility of the Homeowner

A developer of large complexes once told me that an association—any association—only needed one rule. If members observed that one simple rule, there would be no need for any other rules, no need for enforcement, and no need for government overseeing everything. So what is that one simple rule? "Treat your neighbor with respect."

That's it, but unfortunately Donny Osmond was wrong when he sang, "One bad apple doesn't spoil the whole bunch . . . girl." I don't know about apples, but one person not abiding by the above rule makes it ineffective, and now a whole slew of rules need to be invented to govern HOAs. And hence, we need our modern-day Rules & Regulations.

Every association has, had, or will have a troublesome homeowner. An old-time comedian, Slappy White, had a joke that went like this: "I just read that one out of four people is mentally unbalanced. Try it. Think of three of your best friends. If they seem alright to you—you're the one." This can apply to your HOA as well.

It's just a fact of community living that there will be someone who doesn't want to abide by the rules or who feels they should apply to everyone else. Your responsibility is to not be that homeowner. That's not to say that you won't have discord and disagreements with your neighbors or the managing powers of your HOA, because chances are good that you will. The idea is to make those problems the exception, not the rule.

And, of course, you don't want to be the troublesome neighbor. Owning a home comes with responsibility. You have a responsibility to your spouse, your family, and possibly the bank. When your home is in a community development, you also have responsibilities to the other members of your community.

Being a good neighbor is hopefully something that comes naturally to most of us. But there are times, situations, or circumstances that make it difficult. These are some steps you can take to make sure you are doing what is expected of you.

HAVE PRIDE IN YOUR HOME.

Having pride in your home also means having pride in your community. At times, this may mean going the extra mile to improve things.

At one meeting, a homeowner was outraged at the condition of the walkways leading to the units. She screamed at the board that it needed to have the walkways cleaned. The board explained that it just didn't have the funds to do this at this time. The homeowner felt that was unacceptable. Another homeowner interjected and said, "Do what I do. I take my broom and I sweep my walkway." She went on, "Sometimes I even do my neighbor's."

Sometimes we may have to pick up the trash in the streets, shut a gate that was left open, or sweep the walkway. It may not be our job, but it is our community, and making it look nice should be everyone's responsibility.

EDUCATE YOURSELF.

I once had a board member contact me because she was upset about a citation that was issued to one of the units in her condo building. The citation was for having storage on the patio, and she wanted the violation rescinded. She said the cardboard boxes were nicely stacked on the patio and even though this was against the rules, it was a silly rule and shouldn't be enforced.

As I was rule enforcement for this property, I explained to her the reasoning for this particular rule. Cardboard boxes don't hold up. Once the boxes get wet, they start falling apart and, worse, become moldy. Cardboard also attracts rodents and roaches. In tight living corridors, it's hard to get rid of these critters once they invade, and they like to spread out and infest neighboring units. Since the boxes were outside, it would be the responsibility of the HOA to eradicate these pesky critters. And lastly, storage on patios is aesthetically unpleasant. It can make the community look junky and lower property values.

The board member responded, "I didn't realize all that." She no longer was upset by the enforcement of the rule, understood the HOA's demands, and went back to the homeowner to ask her to comply for the betterment of the community.

Rules may seem silly, arbitrary, or unnecessary, but usually there is some logic behind them. As a homeowner, it's your responsibility to learn about your HOA and to gather as much information as possible. If you don't like a rule, ask questions about why it was enacted. You may be surprised by what you uncover.

ABIDE BY THE RULES, EVEN IF OTHERS DON'T.

We've talked about the dos and don'ts of HOA living ad nauseam, but the rules affect everyone and can be the downfall of a community. Most HOA lawsuits, fights among neighbors, and overall dysfunction stem from either lax enforcement or ignoring the rules.

One common argument for not observing the rules is that "no one follows the rules" or "so and so is doing it." This argument doesn't hold water for a number of reasons. You may see someone who is blatantly breaking the rules, but that doesn't mean the association isn't working to remedy the situation. It may be sending letters, calling the homeowner to hearings, and imposing fines, and the homeowner may simply be looking the other way.

Another flaw with this argument is that the board and management may not know about the infraction. Once they are made aware of it, they can take the appropriate action.

One homeowner tried this tactic when called to a hearing for a potential fine. She said her neighbor had the same violation, and she asked him if he had ever been called to a hearing. He told her no. We couldn't share the information with this homeowner, but her neighbor had been called to numerous hearings and was being fined on an ongoing basis. Word of mouth sometimes isn't the most accurate information.

Another way to look at this is if I got ticketed by a police officer for going through a stop sign, my defense of "I drive this street all the time and nobody ever stops at the stop sign" wouldn't get me very far. And it doesn't work with your HOA either. You have the responsibility to know and abide by the rules, regardless of what others are doing. If you truly feel a rule is unfair or is not being enforced properly, then you should address those issues with the board.

PAY DUES IN A TIMELY FASHION.

Associations rely on income from the monthly assessments to function smoothly. If a number of homeowners skip paying their assessments, then the HOA has trouble paying its bills.

When I first started working with HOAs, I had one client that had about 10% of its homeowners who stopped paying their assessments due to an ongoing legal matter. I showed up at one meeting, and the manager told me to leave because they had no money to pay me. I told her I was there and they were going to be charged whether I did the work or not, so I might as well do it and the association could pay me when the situation improved. Things did improve, I got paid, and twenty years later, I'm still working for them. But many vendors—whether individuals or companies working for the association—are not willing or able to extend credit.

Financial hardship for your HOA can result in loss of reputable vendors, services, and amenities. Associations are part of a tight-knit group, and once an association has a reputation for not being able to pay invoices, it's hard to recover. Vendors are reluctant to work for those associations.

Unfortunately, though, most of us have faced hard economic times. Jobs are lost, unexpected circumstances come up, and life sometimes hits below the belt. Understandably at those times, keeping your house out of foreclosure, putting food on the table, and educating your children are top priorities.

Many people in this situation put their HOA last. This can be a mistake for a number of reasons. First, just like the bank, your HOA can foreclose on your property. It's a slower process, but it can and has been done. Second, if you are behind in your assessments, the HOA may file a lien, which is a legal claim filed over your property for a specified amount of money that is paid to the lien holder when the property sells. A lien on the property can make it difficult for the owner to refinance or get a loan. In accordance with the lien, the HOA may turn the file over to a collection agency. Both situations will result in additional fees being added to your account and increases your debt to the association. These fees accumulate quickly and can reach thousands of extra dollars in no time. These costs are usually hard costs to the association, meaning the HOA has to pay them whether you do or not. Homeowners attempting to get current on their bill will ask the HOA to waive these fees, but in most cases, the HOA can't honor that request because it has already paid out these amounts.

The association can also suspend your voting and common area privileges for nonpayment of assessments. This means you won't be able to use any of the recreational facilities like the pool, gym, or clubhouse. If you live in a gated community that has easy access for residents, you may be denied this convenience and forced to use the guest lane every time you go home. The association can't block ingress and egress to your home, but it doesn't have to make it easy for you. In addition, you won't be allowed to vote in the elections and may be unable to serve on the board. If you rent your home, these restrictions apply to your tenant as well.

A homeowner who ignores the suspension and is caught using any of the privileges that have been denied is subject to fines, which, of course, will make the amount you owe even more.

The good news is that your HOA is probably the most sympathetic debtor you will face. These are your neighbors, and they don't want to see you suffer. Although the board has the responsibility to protect the HOA, it is willing to help you. And it's better for it to be getting some money coming in than none at all.

If you find yourself in a financial pickle, here are some steps to take:

- **Reach out to your HOA immediately.** Even before you miss a payment, if possible. Contact management and ask to have a meeting with the board. In most cases, discussions regarding a delinquent account are done in Executive Session, which is a meeting with just the board members and management. This way, you can discuss your situation without it becoming public knowledge. If the policy of your board is to address these matters in Open Session, request to be heard in Executive Session to avoid airing your situation to the whole community.

- **Try to address the issue as quickly as possible.** The previous step was to reach out to your HOA, but that should be done as soon as you become aware there is a problem. Don't wait. The further in the collection process you are, the harder it will be to resolve the issue. In some cases, when the matter is turned over for collection, the board can no longer discuss it with you. You have to deal directly with the collection company, and that can cost more and be more troublesome.

- **Explain the situation honestly to the board.** Financial troubles are embarrassing, but sugarcoating or hiding the situation doesn't help. That doesn't mean you have to reveal all your creditors or verify your income. But let your board know truthfully what is going on.
- **Pay what you can.** If you can make only a partial payment, make it. Not only does every little bit help, but it also shows that you are making an effort and taking the matter seriously.
- **If you are currently behind on your assessments, come up with a payment plan.** Put in writing the amount that you can pay each month to reduce the delinquency. If you can make a large deposit, consider doing that. The board will need to approve any payment plan. Don't be surprised if the board denies your request but presents you with a counteroffer.
- **Don't make promises you can't keep.** Don't offer to pay $500 a month if you can't afford it. Although your intentions may be good, it may be better to offer $400 or a lower amount that won't be as much of a stretch for you. If you do miss a payment, it will only expedite the collection process. The board may also be reluctant to enter into another agreement if you default on your first payment plan. If for some reason you are unable to make your scheduled payment, contact the board *before* it is missed and try to work out an alternate payment plan.
- **Keep the board informed.** Periodically notify the board of your situation. Chances are you aren't going to be able to erase the debt on your account overnight. The board knows it will be a process, but during that process, try to keep your board updated. If you are out of work and gain employment, let the board know. You want your board to be aware of the efforts you are making, and the HOA wants to know that it isn't being ignored or forgotten.
- **Be respectful of the association's position.** The HOA has to think of itself and its members. Nonpaying members are a burden, and even though your intentions may be good, the HOA needs to take steps to ensure its interests are protected. I was a consultant for one HOA that was working with a delinquent homeowner. He would enter into payment plans and then renege. Finally, the HOA sent a letter saying it was filing a lien. The homeowner responded, "I can't pay you. Stop asking me to, and don't send me any more harassing letters." His response was inappropriate and also ineffective, as the association did place a lien on his property.

Remember that it is not the fault of the association that you are in this predicament. Most HOAs will work with you, but you have to be mindful of the situation that they are in as well.

- **Relax.** Talking to your board and dealing with your HOA may be the easiest step you take to get back on your feet financially, so take a deep breath and relax. Chances are good your HOA will work with you in resolving your issue.

COMMUNICATE.

Whether you have a complaint, a request, a question, or a suggestion, it's your job to communicate that to the powers that be. In today's modern age of security cameras, smartphones, social media, and all the other high-tech gadgets and technology, we sometimes assume people know everything. Often, this isn't the case.

If you see a situation that needs attention, report it. Don't assume that someone else will. It's better to be safe than to let a situation continue undetected. Provide as much information as you can in order to facilitate the action needed.

It's also important to communicate in the best manner possible. Sometimes people will wait until the Open Forum at a board meeting to report a maintenance item that can be corrected quickly. Waiting until the meeting can delay the repair or action needed.

MAINTAIN DOCUMENTS PERTAINING TO YOUR PROPERTY.

Even before you close escrow, the paperwork will begin to mount. You get governing documents, deeds, and all kinds of other information. But during your tenure, the paperwork will continue to grow. Some of these notices are informational and can be discarded, but other items should be maintained for the duration of ownership in your property.

Although management should maintain most of these documents, it's a good idea to keep your own copy. Over the years, management may change and things may get lost. There are times when you need documentation, and you don't want to rely on someone else to protect your property. In addition to the governing documents, here are other items you may want to keep.

Year-End or Annual Disclosures

Every November, your HOA is required to send out the Year-End Disclosures. This is a package of materials that contains information about the condition of your association, pertinent data that homeowners may need, and some of the protocols that affect you. The contents of this package may be useful to you throughout the year. Some of the following items are included in your Year-End package:

- **The budget for the upcoming year.** This will give you an idea of where your funds are going and the financial condition of your HOA.
- **Reserve Summary.** This gives an overview of the current conditions of your reserves. The Reserves is an account separate from your operating account that is designated for repair, maintenance, and replacement of common area components. The idea of the Reserves is to guarantee that the association has enough money put away so maintenance, repairs, and replacement of its elements won't bankrupt the HOA. The Reserve Summary is usually generated by an outside source that compiles your Reserve Study. (We'll talk more about the Reserve Study in the "Purpose of the Board" chapter.) Based upon this, they will make a recommendation on the condition of your Reserves and give a "percentage funded" figure. This is the percentage of funds your association needs at this moment based upon the life expectancy of the components. As an example, let's say your association owns a wall and the life expectancy of the wall is ten years and the cost to replace the wall is $1,000. The reserve study determines there are five years left on that wall, therefore you should have $5,000 in your reserves set aside for it. If your reserves are only showing $2,500, then you are 50% funded. This is just an example, and the amount funded figure that is given to you takes into account all components of your HOA. Anything over 70% is pretty darn good. Anything under 50% needs attention. The summary will also suggest how much your association should be contributing to the Reserves on a monthly basis and if a special assessment may be needed to replenish the Reserves.
- **Summary of Insurance.** This is a list of the current insurance policies your HOA has in place and the limits associated with each policy.
- **Collection/Lien Policy.** This explains the process the HOA can take if you become delinquent in your assessments.
- **Payment Information.** This is where you should send your payment each

month. It may also include information on how you can utilize automatic payments. Most HOAs will send out statements for the monthly dues, but this is a courtesy. You are required to pay your assessments on time and in full regardless of whether or not a statement was sent or received.

- **Rule Enforcement.** This is the policy the association follows to encourage compliance with the Rules and Regulations.
- **Dispute Resolution Policies.** There are different methods for dispute resolutions, and this information provides you with the options available to you.
- **Address and Notification Requirements.** These are forms that allow you to have information sent to additional addresses, allow for electronic notifications, opt out of mailing lists, etc.

When you get this bundle at the end of the year, it's a good practice to review it and fill out any needed paperwork. Then file it away. The documents may come in handy during the course of the year. Management can provide you with this information, but it's a good idea to have it readily available if needed.

Minutes

Although you should read the minutes from the board meeting, you don't need to keep every copy. But if there is a mention of your individual unit or anything that affects your property, specifically or generally, you should retain it in your own files. Some HOAs will approve Architectural Request Forms in the Open Session of a board meeting. If your request is discussed, keep these minutes (or at least the page that refers to your request) as proof that you submitted the appropriate form and a record of the board's decision. Other times, there may be a project that will affect your property. For your own purposes, you should keep these minutes.

One homeowner became aware of how important this could be when her HOA decided to add speed humps to try to curtail speeders. One hump was going to be placed right outside her window. The homeowner was advised to not only attend the board meetings where this matter would be discussed but also keep all documentation regarding this installation just in case there were any problems once the speed humps were installed.

In the end, there were problems. It turned out that the placement created a situation at night when cars drove over the hump. The headlights would reflect directly into her unit. She had maintained her documents and was able to present a thorough argument to the board for relocating the speed hump, which it did.

Communications from Management

It's not necessary to keep every letter or email you receive from management. Like the minutes, you should keep any communication that gives approval or specific instructions for your individual property.

A good reason to keep these documents is that if questions arise in the future regarding your property, you don't have to rely on anyone else for the history. There's a side point that is worth mentioning here: when you submit an architectural request, your association has to respond. Some governing documents give a specific timeframe in which the HOA has to get back to you. If they don't respond during that time, or if the governing documents are silent and the HOA doesn't respond in a "reasonable" amount of time, the plans are approved. Some associations will use the silence as the approval process. If the plans are OK, they simply don't respond.

If this is the practice of your HOA, or if you are proceeding with plans without getting a written response, I recommend that you send a quick email to the management company. Simply state the project and summary of details: "In regards to the Architectural Request Submittal to paint the exterior stucco at 123 Main Street, we did not receive a response within the thirty-day time limit and therefore understand the project is approved and will begin with the painting of our property." Save this email. This way you have something in writing that the project was approved. On occasion, an HOA has sent out a denial that you don't receive, and it may come after you at a later date. With the chain of emails, you now have your own evidence that you were within the rules and notified the association of such. If the association responds to your email that it did send a denial letter, then you can at least address the issues prior to doing all the work. It's just a safeguard to protect you and avoid any surprises later on.

Any type of approval should be kept the entire time you own your home.

Violations

If you receive a violation, you should retain a copy of that as well as any additional letters, fines, or hearing determinations. It's also a good idea to keep any supporting communications you have regarding the violations.

Approvals

Always, always, always—this is so important I'm adding another always—get any type of approval in writing. No matter if you are doing major renovations or just something minor, get the approval and any conditions in writing. Even if you are told approval isn't necessary, put it in black and white.

You don't have to wait for the association to put pen to paper, either. You can do it. Simply send an email, like the one above, that says something like, "Per our conversation today regarding the exterior painting of my home at 123 Main Street, I understand that no formal approval is needed and we will begin the project next week." Now you have a paper trail if any discrepancies pop up. If management responds and says that approval is needed, then you can tackle the matter now and avoid future trouble.

Once you get approval, be sure to keep it. Tuck it away in a file just in case there ever is a problem further down the road. You'd be surprised how these things can rear their ugly heads long after you've forgotten about them.

Just as in any relationship, you are going to have peaks and valleys. You start with a honeymoon period, and then there are times when the rigmarole sets in. This applies to friendships, courting, marriage, and yes, even your HOA.

When you first move in, everything is perfect. You have a great board and wonderful neighbors. But then that trait that you found cute and adorable at first starts to get annoying: The enthusiastic board member becomes a "buttinsky." That eclectic house on the corner becomes an eyesore. These feelings sometimes cause people to give in and become part of the problem. But by keeping tuned into your responsibilities, you can minimize the effects these situations will have on you.

Getting Involved

When my sister bought a home in an HOA, I asked her if she was going to run for the board. She said, "There is no way I will ever serve on the board." On behalf of all the people who work for HOAs, I say, "Thank you." Don't get me wrong—I love my sister, but I also know she wouldn't have the temperament or patience to deal with the minutiae involved in being on a board.

This is not uncommon. Not everyone is cut out to be a board member, and that's OK. If I had to be honest, I'm not sure I would have what it takes to be a director either. Even so, there are many ways that you can get involved and on many different levels. We all have talents and skills that our community could benefit from.

Joining a Committee

Most communities have committees. Committees are groups that focus on one specific area. Some common committees include Landscaping, Social, and Architectural. Unlike the board, these committees don't have the authority to make decisions unless it is expressly given by the board. For example, the Social Committee may be planning a block party for the neighborhood. Instead of having to go to the board for every purchase, the board can authorize the committee to spend up to a certain dollar amount. As long as it doesn't go over that amount, the committee is free to spend as it sees fit.

Committees take over a lot of the legwork for the board. They may do a chunk of the research that the board may not have the time to do. Some HOAs will form a committee when getting ready to tackle a large project like paving or painting the entire community. The committee will research vendors, meet with contractors, develop a scope of work, and review contracts. Once it narrows down the choices, the committee presents its findings, along with a recommendation, to the board. The board authorizes the final contract, but the committee did the prep work.

Some committees—landscaping, architectural, etc.—may be defined in your governing documents. But your board has the authority to establish and staff other committees. These committees can become permanent. Others may be only in effect for the duration of a project or for a specified time. So if you see a need that you feel isn't being met, suggest to the board that it establish a committee to address it.

Of course, if you're going to recommend a committee, be prepared to serve on that committee. During the open forum at one meeting, a homeowner told the board that the community should have a committee to vet contractors and vendors. This group, he explained, would interview different vendors, follow up on their references, and visit their offices. The board liked the idea and asked this homeowner to be on the committee. He responded, "I knew if I brought it up you would want me to serve on the committee, but I just don't have the time." It was a good idea, but not if everyone is too busy to staff the committee.

Often, that's the response that an association gets. Homeowners want a service, but they want someone else to provide it. You may have a great idea, but if you are too busy to tackle it, chances are the same is true for your neighbor. The board is already handling its fair share with the ins and outs of the business, so a reply of "I'm too busy" usually leads to a quick demise of that idea or committee, and the project is forgotten.

Volunteering in Your Community

If you don't want the formality of being on a committee, you can volunteer your services by utilizing a skill or hobby. You may be able to do the monthly newsletter, or update the website, or offer your services to redecorate the clubhouse.

In order to run smoothly, an association needs lots of help. And that assistance needs to come from all its members. Yes, you should volunteer your services, but also don't be afraid to recommend the services of someone else.

If you are aware of someone in your community who is gifted or has special talents that could be a benefit, don't be afraid to broach the topic. One condo complex had a woman who had a knack and a love for gardening. When she retired, her next-door neighbor mentioned to the board that she could really help spruce the place up. The board loved the idea and asked her if she would be willing to walk the property with the landscape service on a monthly basis. During these walks, she gave them her opinion on what they should and shouldn't be planting, what needed to be done, and plans for the future. The landscaper liked it because it gave him direction on providing the HOA with the service they wanted. The homeowner liked it because she was involved with plants and gardening, which she loves. The board liked it because it was one less responsibility that it had to tackle. And the homeowners liked it because they now have grounds that are beautiful.

Sometimes all it takes is an invitation. Of course, the person always has the right to say no. But she or he just might say yes, and that's a win-win.

Being Supportive

Being involved can also be as simple as being supportive. If your HOA hosts a block party, attend it. If you can't attend, let the board know that you like the idea. If your HOA has a newsletter, read it. Visit the website. Do things to let the people who are volunteering their time know that you appreciate their work.

A deterrent for getting involved is the idea that you have to attend the board meetings, something that many people just don't want to do. Some may not have the time to sit at a meeting; others just don't like participating in that kind of forum and find it unpleasant. Serving on a committee doesn't require you to attend board meetings. Committee chairs do need to report to the board, but this can be done via email or a written report. Recommendations can be submitted to management along with any requests for board actions.

Although attending the board meetings isn't mandatory for committee members, as a homeowner, it's a good practice to show up to at least one meeting a year. There are a few reasons for this. One, it lets you see the members of your board and the way they act. They are representing you, and you want to make sure it is in a positive way. It also allows your board members to see you. They get to know you and put a face to a name. And it's a little reminder that you are watching them to make sure they are acting in your best interest.

Probably the most important reason to attend a meeting is that you get a feel for what is going on with your neighborhood. Are there a lot of other homeowners there? Are they happy, or is there something that they are outraged about? Is there a topic that keeps coming up throughout the meeting? Are there important issues being pushed aside? By attending the meeting, you are kept in the loop on future plans for your community. There was a story on the news recently where a couple sold their house because of a decision made by the board of directors. The board voted on a matter that affected this home. The couple said they weren't consulted on this matter and were unable to resolve the issue with the association, so they put their house on the market.

The piece on the news showed only one side, and I'm pretty sure there was more to the story. The couple said they had no knowledge that this action was being taken, but if they had attended a board meeting, it probably had been discussed. The time to argue or to debate the merits of a project isn't after the contract has been signed or the work completed. Then it's too late. One way to learn about issues is to attend the board meetings. This way, concerns can be brought to the board's attention as early in the process as possible—either in person, at a meeting, or in written communication.

I can't say specifically, but if I had to guess, I would venture that the couple in the example above chose not to get involved. They decided not to attend meetings, ignored notices that were sent, and waited until they were impacted. By that time, it was too late.

Being informed doesn't require that you be at every meeting and stay for the duration. You can get the information by requesting and reading your board minutes. These can be mailed to you, or many HOAs are now posting them online. But by attending one meeting and then reading the minutes, you can judge if the minutes are reliable.

It's easy for all of us to think of excuses why we can't participate, but in the end, it's our community and our responsibility. It's the members who will transform an HOA from just an association into a tight-knit neighborhood.

What's Happening in Your HOA?

I was working with one property that was repaving its streets. This was a costly adventure. It took weeks of planning to make sure the homeowners were notified of the street closures, restrictions during the process, and what was expected of the homeowners during the project. Just as one section of the street had been completed, a homeowner pulled his car out of his driveway, through the tape that had been erected, and drove on the newly paved streets. The work was ruined and had to be redone.

The cost for the new work was forwarded to the homeowner. He was shocked. He argued that he wasn't notified and had no other options because he had to get to work, and therefore he shouldn't be responsible for these additional fees. In reality, the association had mailed a notice to each owner and resident, not once but twice, flyers were posted on every entrance gate at the community, an announcement was added to the community website, and the guard handed out a printed flyer with instructions to every vehicle that entered the gates for a week prior. The homeowner's response was, "You didn't expect me to read that junk, did you?"

The short answer is "yes." The HOA has a responsibility to notify you, but you also have a responsibility to make yourself aware of what is happening. Here are some things you can use to be aware and in the know.

Governing Documents

The basic information on your HOA can be found in the governing docs—the CC&Rs, Bylaws, and Rules and Regulations. Check to make sure you have the most up-to-date copy of these, especially the Rules and Regulations, as these tend to be modified more often than the other two.

You can contact your management company and ask if the version you have is the most current. They should be able to tell you if any of the documents have been changed and when. Management may charge you for a hard copy of these documents, but they may have a download option available at a reduced rate or free of charge.

As a homeowner, you want to make sure your CC&Rs, Bylaws, and Rules and Regulations are handy or easily available. You may need to refer to these documents on a regular basis.

Tools or Services

Most associations want members to be "in the know" and have tools in place to do that. Some of these mechanisms include the following:

NEWSLETTERS

Some HOAs have great newsletters. They are well-written, attractive sheets filled with all kinds of useful information. Someone puts in many hours generating this publication, and your association spends money to send it out. Take a few minutes to read the newsletter, especially if there are large projects or issues going on in your neighborhood.

WEBSITE

Your HOA may have its own website or one through its management company. Take a moment to get familiar with this site. Some items on a website may include the governing documents (for easy reference or to download for free or for a minimal fee), announcements of upcoming events that affect homeowners, meeting minutes, forms that a homeowner may need like the Architectural Request Form or a Complaint Form, and information for contacting management or the board. Some websites are even more interactive, and you can access your HOA account, pay your bill, and request a repair or service.

If you have trouble negotiating your community's website, contact your management company. Most management companies want you to utilize these sites and will take the time to walk you through the process. Don't be afraid to ask them for help.

GATE SERVICE

If you live in a gated community, the gate is the access point not only for you but for all your guests. If people can't get through the gate, they aren't going to get to you. Many gates, in order to streamline the process of getting people in and out quickly, have a gate access service. This is a computer-based system that allows you to input information on your guests, vendors, packages, and parties all from the comfort of your home. You enter the information, and when your guest arrives, the guard has everything at the ready. Without this system, every time a guest comes to the community, expected or unexpected, the guard has to contact the homeowner. This can be time consuming, resulting in long lines and wanted guests being turned away.

The gate service will allow you to add permanent guests to your account. These are the people—family and friends—whom you want to give unrestricted access to your home. They are allowed to visit you anytime. You also may be able to add routine vendors like gardeners, the pool man, or cleaning services. You can list the days and times they come, and they will be granted access for only those days. You can also add one-time guests—a person who comes to visit but isn't someone you want to give unlimited access. Some services have an added feature that will send you a text message when your guest arrives. The great thing about these programs is that all that information can be added conveniently using your computer or your cell phone.

These are just some examples of what gate access software can do. Some are very complex and allow for a lot of different features. Find out what services your gate access has, sign up, and use them.

Notifications/Correspondence

When you live in an HOA, you will be getting notifications and correspondence through many avenues. Some communications are required by civil code to be hand delivered or mailed. Email isn't an option. There are other communications that your association may elect to only email in order to save costs. In either case, when you receive something from your association or management company, take a moment to read it.

That sounds so simple, but vital information is often simply ignored. It's easy to do so. The mail comes, and we put it aside until we have time to handle it. And sometimes it just sits. But some of the correspondence from the HOA includes deadlines or important details. In some cases, as with violation hearings, not responding can result in monetary fines being imposed. Make it a practice to open anything from your HOA or management company.

Changes in the Law

Every year, state legislatures make changes that affect you, and often these changes deal directly with HOAs and the way they can conduct business. Most of these new laws take effect on January 1, but occasionally they have a different date that they become active.

When it comes to HOAs, these law amendments can have a big effect on you. As a homeowner, they may give you more freedoms or may create more hoops for you to jump through. In either case, you should know what they are.

States usually have a website and will post what new legislature is going into effect. Towards the end of the year, take a gander and do a quick search. You can also contact your management company. Most HOA law firms will send management companies a summary of new laws that affect the running of an HOA so they can disseminate the information to their clients.

Community Participation

A great way to be aware of what is going on is to be a part of your community. One way to do this is to volunteer for committees and such, as we talked about in the previous chapter. But being a part of your community doesn't necessarily have to be a formal commitment. It can be getting to know your neighbors and just being alert to what is happening. If you see something unusual, ask questions. If you see something in disrepair, report it. Take an interest in what is going on around you.

Meetings

The monthly (or however often your HOA holds them) meetings are a great way to learn what is going on in your community. This is where the board discusses what projects are in the works, what the future plans are, and what issues the HOA is facing. This is a wonderful source of information for homeowners.

If you can't or don't want to attend the board meetings, you can still keep abreast of the news by reading the minutes. A draft of the minutes from a board meeting must be made available to a homeowner within thirty days of the meeting, if requested by the homeowner. Some HOAs will send them out automatically, but they aren't obligated to do so. If your HOA isn't one of those, then you will need to request the minutes, and in some cases, you will have to pay a minimal fee for them. Now more and more HOAs are posting approved minutes on their websites. So if your HOA is not offering this service, ask your board to consider doing this.

When it comes to your HOA, there is no such thing as being too informed. With the tools supplied by your association and a little effort on your part, you can avoid the frustrations of being blindsided by changes in your community. Not being aware of what is going on in your community can cost you time and money. An association can try to inform its members, but each individual has to make his own choice on his level of participation.

Renting My Home

After the turn of the century, our country faced a very challenging time. The lucrative real estate bubble burst. This left some homeowners without income and unable to pay their mortgages and others with an upside-down mortgage.

Someone in this position had few options—foreclosure, a short sale, or renting the property to cover expenses and find more reasonable living accommodations (i.e., mom and dad). The side effect of this economic downturn was that many HOAs found their communities filled with rental properties. Homeowners who couldn't afford to live in a certain community would rent out their homes until things improved and they could move back or the market rebounded and they could sell. The influx of short sales and foreclosures were a bonanza for investors, and many were buying up properties even before they were on the market.

It wasn't uncommon to find a realtor working a community and keeping his or her antennas up for people who were struggling. A conversation would be initiated, and if the homeowner was open to selling, the realtor would offer to find a buyer—usually an investor that he or she knew would buy anything within a certain price range—and negotiate with the bank to accept the lower price. There was nothing wrong with this practice. In fact, it benefited many homeowners who otherwise would have lost their houses in foreclosure. It also benefited the HOAs because they lost a homeowner who was struggling to pay his or her assessments and gained one who was able to write a check to the HOA every month.

This trend has continued, and the large number of rental properties has an effect on associations. In some cases, there are properties that were previously 90% owner occupied but now are finding that more than half the units in a complex are rented.

Renting a unit is not automatically a bad thing. There are some tenants who are wonderful. They have lived in the unit for a long time, abide by the rules, and respect both the landlord's property and the common area. But many tenants are just the opposite, and this is what causes some HOAs concern.

If you plan on renting your unit either long-term or just for a short period of time, here are some things to consider.

Governing Documents

Before entering into a lease on your unit, be sure to review the governing documents. Many CC&Rs have restrictions on renting a unit. It's not uncommon for the CC&Rs to ban short-duration rentals and dictate the actual length of a lease. It may also require a written lease and limit the number of people who can reside in your unit. You may be required to provide certain information—like names of residents, vehicles, pets, etc.—to the association within a specified time frame.

Although not as common, some HOAs are limited in the number of units that can be rented at one time. If your HOA is at that threshold, you won't be able to rent your unit until a space opens up. You are put on a waiting list. When your number comes up, you'll have a certain amount of time to rent your unit or you move to the end of the line again.

Another condition that some associations have is that the unit must be owner occupied for a certain period of time after purchase. It may be as short as few months, but a few years is more common. This means if you haven't owned your unit for that amount of time, you are prohibited from renting it out.

Before making the commitment to rent out your property, you want to read your CC&Rs for any mention of leasing a unit. You also want to review the Rules and Regs, as there may be other restrictions you have to follow. Then you can make an informed decision on becoming a landlord.

Since we're talking about the CC&Rs and the Rules and Regs . . . make sure your tenants have a copy of these documents. Some associations will make you sign a statement that you have supplied these to your renters, and they have to sign that they received them. Just as with homeowners, not knowing the rules isn't an acceptable excuse for not following them.

Responsibility for Your Tenants/Guests

I recently had an argument with a landlord who was cited for something his tenant did and wanted the HOA to pursue it with his tenant. I told him it didn't work that way. The HOA's contract is not with his tenant but with him. He argued, "My tenant broke the rules and he's an adult, therefore you need to go after him. I'm not responsible for another person's actions."

I asked, "If your tenant decided to not renew his lease and you discovered he spray-painted obscenities on the living room wall, would you give him his security deposit back?"

"Absolutely not," was the response.

"But what if he says it was a guest who did the artwork? That person was an adult and the tenant isn't responsible for his actions. Would you give him his security back and pursue it with the friend?"

"He's bound by the lease, which says he's responsible."

Exactly. The homeowner was bound by the CC&Rs, which stated the homeowner is responsible for his tenant and their guests. A landlord can't expect to transfer the burden of his tenants to the association.

Most CC&Rs will have a clause that is similar to this one: "Any unit owner who shall lease his or her unit to any person(s) or entity shall be responsible for assuring compliance by any such person(s) or entity with all of the covenants, conditions, restrictions, easements, as amended and supplemented." This means the HOA will go after you for the actions of your tenant.

As a landlord, you are also responsible for any actions of your tenant's guests. The governing documents typically have a clause that say something like: "Unit owner is responsible for any damage to any real or personal property in the association caused by an owner, owner occupant (lease), or invitee." This also applies to homeowners—you can be held accountable for your guests' actions.

If your tenant or his or her guests damage the common area in any way, the cost of repair will be added to your HOA account. It will be up to you to recoup your losses from the tenant, so be sure your lease covers you on this matter.

I've seen many first-time landlords get burned when their tenant racks up a slew of monetary fines with the HOA. When they tried to get the funds from their renter, they found out this wasn't covered in the lease and they weren't able to collect. Be sure your lease protects you in case your tenant turns out to be less than stellar.

And that does happen. One gentleman lived in a unit for eight years. During that time, he was a role model as far as tenants go. He obeyed the rules, was courteous to his neighbors, and actually was an asset to the community. Then he decided to terminate his lease and move away, and everything changed. He stopped paying his rent, the rules went out the window, and in just a couple of months, he racked up over a thousand dollars in fines. The icing on the cake was his final action as a tenant. Right before he vacated the unit, he sued the landlord. I don't know what happened with the lawsuit, but I do know the HOA collected from the owner on all the fines.

The Business of Renting

MANAGE YOUR TENANTS.

When you lease your unit, you technically become a business. It is your job to manage your tenants, their complaints and their concerns, or hire someone to do it for you. The association, the board, and the management aren't going to monitor or oversee the residents of your unit.

In most cases, the HOA is going to continue to communicate with you, as you are the member of the association. This means letters and communications are going to be sent to you, and it is your job to inform the residents of your unit. Some communities require that any requests for service come through you.

Tenants may also be restricted from participating at the board meetings. Again, these are member meetings, and although a tenant lives in the community, they are not a member of the HOA. Each complex has different rules on tenants attending meetings. Some restrict it completely, others will allow tenants to attend but not to speak, and others permit tenants to attend only if accompanied by the homeowner.

My recommendation to boards who ask if tenants can participate at meetings is to allow their attendance, with the condition that the homeowner submits written permission to the HOA. This can just be a quick email that gives authorization to the tenant to attend meetings for the duration of the tenancy. This provides the HOA a little bit of insurance if for some reason the landlord-tenant relationship takes a bad turn. The homeowner can't come back to the association and say, "Why did you discuss these matters in front of my tenant?"

If you want your tenant to be able to vote, take action, and represent all your rights with the association, then you may want to consider giving him or her power of attorney. This is something you should give thought to and maybe even consult with an attorney, as this is a legal step and may have other implications.

RUN YOUR TENANCY LIKE A BUSINESS.

There is more involved with renting a unit than simply collecting the rent check each month. It is a business and should be treated as such.

As the landlord, you are the one who will need to make necessary repairs, maintain the property, and be the liaison between the HOA and the tenant. If you can't do this job, you can hire someone to manage the property for you. It's not the job of the association's management company to supervise your tenant.

Whether you do it yourself or hire a service, you will need to keep the association informed of any changes in tenancy. You should know who is in your unit, have their contact information, and provide your tenants with the information they need to be respectable residents.

MAINTAIN INSURANCE AND REQUIRE YOUR TENANT TO HAVE RENTER'S INSURANCE.

Even though you won't be living in the unit, it is still a good idea to maintain appropriate insurance. Speak with an agent and find out what policies you should carry. You want to make sure you and your property are protected against theft, fire, disasters, and even vengeful tenants.

The policy that the HOA has covers the association property. One agent described it by saying, "Imagine you could pick up the unit on the day the developer turned it over to the association, flip it upside down, and shake it. The association's insurance covers the stuff that doesn't fall out." This means the walls, the floor, attached fixtures, etc., but not the belongings. You want to have adequate insurance that will restore your unit to its current condition. For example, many HOA insurance policies don't include upgrades. This means if you've installed hardwood flooring and there is a claim, you may only get reimbursement for standard carpeting. Even if you don't rent your unit, it's a good idea to consult with an insurance agent to make sure you have adequate coverage for your personal property, loss assessment, and upgrades.

It's also a good idea, and in some HOAs a requirement, to insist your tenants have their own renter's insurance. This policy won't protect the shell of the unit, but it provides coverage on the tenant's personal property in case of a water leak or some destructive incident. This kind of policy will help protect both you and the association.

Hopefully it will never be needed, but when something goes wrong, having all the appropriate insurance in place is one less thing to worry about.

Being Involved

CHECK ON YOUR UNIT OR HAVE SOMEONE IN THE COMMUNITY CHECK ON THE PROPERTY.

One reason rental properties get a bad reputation has to do with absentee owners/landlords. Absentee doesn't have anything to do with location but rather with attitude. There are landlords who live on the other side of the country from where their property is but still manage to be an interested party in the operations of their unit. And there are owners who live within walking distance and couldn't be bothered with anything having to do with the property—except cashing the rent check every month.

I was at one hearing where an owner attended because his tenant was cited for multiple violations. He was there to represent his tenants, who claimed they were being harassed. At one point, he asked for all the violations on his unit, which included leaving a dog on the patio. He said, "I have to stop you right there. My tenants don't have a dog, so obviously you're mistaken." I gave him the picture I had just taken an hour before the meeting. The board members told him that the family he rented to had had the dog for over a year.

The owner was stunned. He said, "I guess I'm going to have to come around here a little more often." The board president told him it would be worthwhile for him to stop by periodically to see for himself what was going on, even if he had to make a special trip. He responded, "Oh, it won't be that hard; I live just around the corner."

VISIT YOUR PROPERTY.

Make your presence known both to the renters in the unit as well as to the association. You want to be sure your property is being maintained and cared for. There have been incidents where tenants have done some pretty nasty things to the unit. Landlords show up for the final walkthrough and are devastated by the amount of destruction. At this point, the tenant may be long gone and the owner bears the cost of restoring the property.

Come by and let your tenants and the association know you still have an interest in your property. If you can't do it, ask a friend to keep an eye on the place. Tenants may be on better behavior if they think you may just pop by, and if the HOA sees you are still involved with the community, they may be more inclined to share with you anything that seems out of the ordinary.

Renting out your property can be a viable opportunity for you and doesn't have to be an inconvenience to the HOA. I've witnessed it being done successfully many times. With the proper planning, effort, and forethought, you can get the monthly income you need and want. And the association gets a welcomed addition to the community. Ideally, it can be a win-win.

PART TWO

THE BOARD

Who Is the Board?

The simple definition of an HOA's board of directors is the people the membership elects to run your corporation.

If you want to understand the who, what, where, and why of your board, the best place to start is with your Bylaws. This is where you will find the boundaries or procedures you have to follow for your election, requirements for becoming board members (if any), and the makeup of your board. The Bylaws should tell you how many board members you must have, the requirements for a quorum, and the board positions or officers.

Positions on the Board

The board is made up of a specified number of directors. Most HOAs will have five directors, although larger communities may have more and small associations may have less. Usually the number will be an odd amount in order to reduce the likelihood of a tie vote.

The board members, or directors, are the people you elect to the board. Among your elected board, you will have officers—or, as they may be called, "board positions." Common officer positions are president, vice president, secretary, and treasurer. All other directors become members-at-large.

The board decides on these positions among themselves, and they are not voted on by the homeowners. On very rare occasions, a person can be an officer but not a member of the board. This person fulfills the duties of the assigned position but doesn't have voting power on the board of directors.

Unlike directors, officers can be removed by a simple vote of the board. They serve at the board's discretion.

PRESIDENT

The president is the chairperson of your board. Typical duties for the president are overseeing or chairing the board and membership meetings. The president can call a meeting of the board at his or her sole discretion. All other board members need two or more members of the board to concur in order to hold a meeting. In either case, all other criteria for holding a meeting must be met.

The president is usually the liaison between management and the board and commonly is the contact person for the association's attorney.

The Bylaws may grant the president more specific duties, and the board members may vote to give the president additional leeway in certain situations. For example, the board may vote to allow the president to use his or her discretion to approve small expenditures to facilitate the running of the HOA as a business. These privileges should be spelled out in a formal motion in the minutes that list their limitations. Any authorizations bestowed on the president are at the discretion of the board. If other board members feel the president is overstepping his or her boundaries, they have the right to rescind these privileges with a majority vote.

Since the president is usually the most prominent and vocal position on the board, some people believe it carries more power. This isn't really true. All board members, regardless of their position, have one equal vote. The president's vote doesn't carry more punch than those of the members-at-large.

This brings up another common fallacy—that is, that the president can't make or vote on motions. On some boards—mostly corporate—this is the case. The president has a vote only when it is needed to break a tie. On HOA boards, every member is given one vote regardless of their position. During a vote, the president can exercise his or her right to vote, or he or she may choose to withhold his or her vote in case there is a tie. It is completely up to the president how to handle his or her vote. What is not allowed is for the president to cast a vote that results in a tie and then cast another vote as the tiebreaker. Being appointed president or any other position doesn't remove a director's right to vote, but the president is only allotted one vote, the same as all the other directors.

VICE PRESIDENT

There is an old joke—"The Vice President has the easiest job in the country: all he has to do is to wake up every morning and say, 'How's the President?'" This applies to your board of directors as well. The duty of the vice president is to fill in if the president is unable to do so. If the president can't attend a meeting, the vice president will assume the role of the chair and run the meeting. Other than that, the duties of the VP are the same as those of every other board member.

TREASURER

As you can guess, the treasurer is the association's money person. This doesn't mean that the treasurer has unlimited access to the HOA's funds. It means that the person in this position has the task of reviewing the group's accounts.

Most HOAs have either an independent accountant or the management prepare the financial statements on a monthly basis. It is required that the board reviews these documents on a quarterly basis, but it is encouraged to do so more frequently. The treasurer is the board member who reviews the documents and notes any unusual activity.

He or she also oversees all the other issues pertaining to the association's finances. This includes investments, taxes, reserve study, and budget. The treasurer doesn't need to have a background in finance, but it does help.

SECRETARY

The secretary is the custodian of the HOA's written documents. The secretary is responsible for posting the meeting notices and agenda, although it's not unusual for this to be done by the management company. Members have a right to certain documents, and it is the job of the secretary to make sure those documents are available to be duplicated or inspected. Once again, this is usually delegated to the management company. This way, all paperwork is in one central location.

The secretary is also responsible for taking and preparing the meeting minutes, although this task is generally outsourced to an independent contractor, like me, or management. This person will attend the meetings and generate minutes for the board to approve. I worked with one board where a homeowner agreed to be the secretary but only on the condition that I attend the meetings to take the minutes. He gave me his phone number and said, "If you can't make it to a meeting, call me, because if you're not there, I'm not going to be there." Many board members don't want the task of taking minutes and, luckily for me and my bank account, this is a job that is allowed to be subbed out.

In addition, the secretary has the task of signing official HOA documents along with the president. These may include foreclosures, legal documents, and the finalized version of the meeting minutes. The secretary also maintains the association's official documents, although again, this is usually done by the management in order to have all documents in one place and easily accessible. This lowers the risk of losing important docs.

Some governing documents will stipulate that the secretary is the point person for notification of the HOA. Homeowners may submit information to this person, as the secretary, and it is considered formal notification to the HOA. This may include petitions, architectural requests, changes of addresses, and other items when homeowners need to notify the association.

Electing Your Board

As we said earlier, board positions or officers are at the discretion of the board and are appointed by the board members. The board can remove or replace officers with a majority vote of the board members, and this may be done whenever the board feels it is necessary.

A board is elected at the Annual Meeting or Members Meeting. Most HOAs are required to hold an election every year, even though all board members may not be up for re-election every year. Some governing documents specify exactly when your association must hold its election. It will give the exact day, time, and place when the meeting must be held. More common is simply that the election must be held on an annual basis and will allow the board to pick a date that is convenient for the membership.

NOMINATING CANDIDATES

In recent years, association elections have gone through some major changes. In California, all HOA board of director elections have to be done by secret ballots. This is the process for how HOA elections are carried out today: First, a nomination form is sent out to the membership. Members who are interested in serving on the board can submit the form to have their name added to the ballot. As a homeowner, you can also nominate another member whom you feel will be a good addition to the board. If you do submit someone, be sure to get their permission.

Some associations will also allow you to write in candidates on the ballot. This allows you to vote for someone who forgot to or didn't submit their name in time. Again, only write in people who you know want to be a part of the board.

In one election, there was a homeowner who owned quite a few units and therefore had multiple ballots. Each ballot allowed him five votes. He decided to nominate different people and wrote in twenty-five different names as candidates on his ballots, giving each person one vote. At the end of the election for five board members, the HOA had four board members and twenty-five people tied for the fifth position. The manager had to contact each member and find out if he or she was willing to accept the position. If the candidate said no, he or she was crossed off the list; if the candidate said yes, he or she was added to the slate for a runoff election. It ended up taking four months to fill one seat. You can avoid this kind of conflict by simply asking the person, "Would it be OK if I put your name on the ballot?" If the person says "no" or shows no interest in serving on the board, then don't write in that person's name. The person may be an asset to the board, but he or she can't be forced to serve.

Nomination forms will need to be submitted by a certain date, so be sure to observe the deadlines. If you miss the deadline and still want to run for the board, you will need to attend the meeting when the election is being held and add your name as a nomination from the floor, if this is permitted per your governing documents. The drawback to this method is that ballots have already been mailed in, so the only votes you may get are from the homeowners who attend the meeting. Often, few homeowners attend the actual meeting, as they are allowed and prefer to cast their vote by mail.

BALLOTS

Once the nomination forms are returned, the ballots are sent out. These are sent with a secret ballot envelope and a separate mailing envelope for returning the ballot. Once you fill out the ballot, you will put it in the ballot envelope and seal it. Place the sealed envelope in the mailing envelope and fill out the return information on this envelope. This information will include your name, property address, and a signature. All information has to be filled out for your ballot to count.

The mailing envelope is what is used to make sure the ballot is legitimate and is coming from a member who is eligible to vote. (Some homeowners who are delinquent in their assessments may have their voting privileges suspended and are not allowed to vote in the election.) The mailing envelope contains your information along with a signature, and due to identity theft concerns, some homeowners are reluctant to place it in the mail with this information visible. It's a valid concern, so in this case, follow the above instructions and then enclose the signed, sealed envelope in another envelope and mail it to the address on the ballot. This way the inspector will still have the information needed to verify the ballot, the ballot remains sealed and secret, and your personal information won't be seen until the mailing envelope is opened. The other option is to attend the meeting and bring the ballot with you.

It's also important that you not sign the ballot or include any identifying information on the ballot or in the ballot envelope. At the meeting, the ballot envelopes will be separated from the mailing envelopes. The idea behind the secret ballots is that no one knows how or for whom each member votes.

One helpful homeowner came to an annual meeting and pulled me aside. He said he noticed that the ballots didn't have a space for the homeowner's address and signature. So he went door to door in the community and told everyone to just go ahead and add this information to their ballots. His intentions were well-meant, but unfortunately half of the ballots were disqualified and couldn't be counted in the election.

INSPECTORS OF ELECTION

Prior to the election, Inspectors of Election will need to be appointed, which is done by the board. The Inspectors of Election are one to three people who will oversee the ballots and the election process. In most cases, the Inspectors of

Election are from your management company, but they can be homeowners as long as they or anyone from their home are not on the board or ballot. Or they can be an independent contractor who is hired to conduct the election.

The Inspectors of Election are responsible for accepting and verifying the ballots. They log in each envelope received and make sure the person is eligible to vote. They also make sure that only one ballot per address is received. In HOAs, if duplicate ballots are received, the *earliest* ballot is valid.

The decision of who will be the Inspectors of Election shouldn't be made quickly, because the Inspectors have the right and power to invalidate ballots. They singlehandedly decide if a ballot is counted towards the quorum and/or the election. Any decisions made by the Inspectors of Election are final, and as a homeowner, you have no right to question their reasoning at a meeting.

After a quorum is established, the Inspectors of Election will open the mailing envelopes and separate them from the ballot envelopes. Once this procedure is complete, they will open the ballot envelopes and begin the process of tallying the votes. Homeowners have the right to view this process but not participate, question, or interfere with the Inspectors of Election during it.

Once the votes have been counted, the Inspectors will either read the results or give them to the chair of the meeting to read. A copy of the tally sheet and/or the final results should be signed by the Inspectors. Election results should also be sent to the membership and reported in the minutes of the next board of directors meeting. All paperwork pertaining to the election should be held either by the management company or the vendor hired as the Inspector of Elections. Homeowners have the right to review the paperwork if they submit a written request and make arrangements through management. An election can be contested for one year following the election.

QUORUM

In order to hold the meeting, you need to establish a quorum. This is the minimum number of people needed to open the meeting and conduct business. At the annual meeting, homeowners make up the quorum, and that is achieved through ballots that have been submitted. The Bylaws will dictate the number of ballots you need to hold the election. Usually this is 50% of the membership plus one. For example, if your HOA has one hundred members, you need fifty-one ballots in order to call the meeting to order and to proceed with the election. Although 50% plus one is the most common, there are some HOAs that require a larger number and some that allow for a smaller one.

VOTING

Your Bylaws will determine the method of voting that is used in your HOA. You may have cumulative voting, where you are given a vote for each board position that is up for election. If there are five seats up for election, then you have five votes. You can cast your votes in any method you like, provided it adds up to five and there are no fractional votes. This means if you have five open seats and five people running, you can give each person one vote, or two to one person and three to another, or you can allocate all five votes to one person. You also have the option not to cast any votes at all, in which case your ballot still counts towards the quorum, but you choose to not vote for any candidate on the ballot.

Here is an example of cumulative voting:

There are five (5) positions up for election, therefore you have five (5) votes. You may cast all your votes for one candidate or divide your votes in any manner among candidates. If your ballot contains an excess of five (5) votes, or fractional votes, none of such votes will be counted and the ballot voided.

Nominees	Votes
(1) Sophia Adams	3
(2) Karen Jones	
(3) Dean Johns	
(4) Mario Nichols	1
(5) Tom Warren	1

Another method is simply that every unit gets one vote. You cast your single vote for whichever candidate you choose, no matter how many seats are up for election. The persons with the most votes are elected. If there are three open seats, the top three vote-getters are elected to the board.

Prior to the implementation of the current election system, proxies were a big part of the voting in HOAs and a large source of contention. Nowadays, proxies don't play as big a role in the process, and some HOAs don't allow them at all. Homeowners can vote without attending the meeting, making the need for proxies unnecessary.

Should You Serve on Your Board?

Usually when someone is asked to serve on a board, their first response is, "What qualifications do I need?" With HOAs, the answer is pretty simple: you need to be a member, and sometimes not even that. Yes, it's hard to believe, but some HOAs allow people to serve on their board who have no vested interest in the community at all. They don't have to reside in the community; they don't have to be a member of the association. The only qualification is that they don't have a criminal record and are willing to do the job.

This, though, is rare. Most HOAs require that in order to serve on a board, you have to be a member of the community. Your Bylaws should also spell out the requirements for membership. The usual definition is that you have to be listed on the title of the property, but there are some cases where the lines get blurred. You may have a husband and wife where only one is listed on the title, or parents may buy the unit for a son or daughter. In some cases, the property is owned by a corporation or trust. In these cases, you may need to get the advice of an attorney.

Some associations are even more restrictive: you not only have to be a member but also a member in good standing. This means you can't be delinquent in any manner and that your voting privileges haven't been suspended for violations or other behavior. And some HOAs will require that you not only be a member but also reside in the community.

Generally, the only requirements are that you are a member, that you haven't been convicted of a felony, that you are willing to do the job, and that someone in the community votes for you.

Should you serve on your board is a different question and one that only you can answer. The idealistic answer is, "Of course, everyone should serve on their neighborhood board." But the realistic answer is that some people really shouldn't.

This isn't a personal attack against anyone, but there are reasons why volunteering for a board isn't the best idea. In the upcoming chapter, "Good Board, Bad Board," we talk about good and bad boards, and each person has to decide for themselves if they would be a benefit or a hindrance to the board. One reason that you might not be the best candidate for a spot on the board is if you have a heavy, inflexible work schedule. You can't ask someone to give up their paying job for a volunteer position. Attendance at board meetings and accessibility during the month by email are a must. You shouldn't be on a board if doing so is going to put your job at risk. Wait until your situation changes, and then you can consider running.

The same goes with your home life. Kids have soccer practice, tutoring sessions, piano lessons, karate, Girl Scouts, and someone has to drive them to all these places. And of course, they need food, clean clothes, and to get homework done. These are valid—and wonderful—reasons for not being able to commit to a position on the board. When your kids get older and need you less, you may be able to find the time.

I was the recording secretary for one HOA whose board president tried to hold a board meeting during her daughter's soccer practice. It wasn't successful. Her daughter wasn't happy, the other board members weren't thrilled, and I went home with a whole bunch of mosquito bites. That was the one and only time she did that. A short time after that, the president resigned from the board. She realized she couldn't do it all.

Be honest in your evaluation of whether or not you can serve on a board. You may have the right aptitude and ethics for the job, but extenuating circumstances may prevent you from serving . . . for now.

Purpose of the Board

A board of directors has one main purpose, and that is to run your HOA. Generally, an HOA is a nonprofit corporation. Just like any business, it brings money in and expends money out. And like any business, its goal is to make sure it has more money coming in than going out. That responsibility falls on your board of directors.

Unlike other businesses, positions on the board of directors are completely voluntary. They don't get a salary. They don't get any kind of compensation, not even a reduction in their monthly assessment.

Your CC&Rs and Bylaws may state that your board members must be volunteers. If a board receives compensation for performing board duties, they lose the protection of the volunteer status. In some rare cases, you may be forced to have a professional board member (court order) or be allowed to through special circumstances. In order to have a "professional board member" (i.e., someone who is paid either with a salary or other compensation), the association may be required to obtain different insurance. The individual will also need to maintain his or her own personal insurance to cover actions as a board member.

It is important to be aware of and understand the distinction between a volunteer and a paid, professional board member. Paid board members are not common. In most cases, the only time you will see a professional board member is when he or she is appointed by a court. This is done when an HOA is in such disarray that no one in that association is willing to serve on the board. In order to allow the association to continue to function, a judge will appoint someone to the board and dictate an appropriate salary, with the cost being absorbed by the homeowners. Any compensation made to a board member must be disclosed to the membership. Volunteer board members are entitled to reimbursement relating to association expenditures, and this isn't considered compensation.

So basically, your board members earn zero dollars, and they have to work hard for that salary. They wear many hats and have to make decisions that affect not only themselves but also everyone else in the community.

In most cases, the board is doing the best job they can with the restrictions placed on them by the legislature, city ordinances, and your own governing documents. They make decisions in the best interest of the community, and sometimes those decisions go against you. As a homeowner, you have the right to be angry and frustrated and demand action, but no homeowner has the right to be abusive to the board.

Let's take a look at some of the things a board is responsible for.

Maintaining the Reserves

The board is responsible for the fiscal well-being of your HOA. The board drafts, reviews, and approves a budget on a yearly basis. This budget not only includes the operating expenses—insurance, utilities, management fee—but also the reserve allocation.

The Reserves is a separate account or accounts that the association must maintain to cover the common area elements that every HOA has. These can include clubhouses, streets, buildings, plants—basically anything that the association owns that needs to be replaced, repaired, or maintained.

Each HOA is required to prepare a Reserve Study. Although not required, most HOAs will hire an independent company to prepare the Reserve Study. The company will come to your property, take pictures, and prepare a detailed summary of all the components of your association along with their values, estimated life span, and remaining life. The report also estimates the funds needed to maintain these elements. The figures in the Reserve Study are estimates based on mathematical formulas using industry standards, but they give the board members an idea of what is needed to preserve the community.

The report will also suggest how much the HOA should be putting into the Reserve account on a monthly or annual basis. It is the board's responsibility to review this report to make sure it is inclusive and to determine how to best fund the Reserves. The board is required to review the Reserve Study on an annual basis. Associations are mandated to have a Reserve Study with a site visit completed every three years. A lot of HOAs will choose to have an update done each year, usually in preparation of their budget.

Well-funded reserves are crucial to your HOA. Without solid reserves, common area elements tend to be neglected. This can make the community look rundown and is aesthetically unpleasing. Low reserves can affect your association's insurance premiums, as components that aren't maintained can potentially result in more insurance claims.

Homes in underfunded associations also have a harder time getting mortgages because the chances for special assessments are higher. This makes banks nervous and may affect property values, refinancing options, VA loans, FHA status, and standard loans from the bank.

As a result, maintaining healthy reserves should be a goal of every board.

Community Maintenance

Along this same line is the maintenance of your community. Your board has the job of making sure that repairs and preventive maintenance are done correctly and in a timely fashion.

The board, with the assistance of management and sometimes hired professionals, will determine a schedule of necessary repairs and upgrades. The list should be prioritized by importance as well as the ability to fund the project. Your board will interview and contract with different vendors in order to maintain the common area elements.

The board is the deciding factor on what projects the association is going to tackle and the timeframe for doing so. When you own a home, there is always a wish list of improvements you would like to make. The same is true for your HOA. And just like in your personal life, those projects can't be done until there is funding. That task lies with your board.

The board would love to do everything the community wants, but it's not always possible. It has to prioritize, plan, and schedule so that projects don't bankrupt the HOA.

Enforcing Rules

The board is the entity that has to enforce all those rules, restrictions, and conditions that we have talked about to maintain order in the community.

There is a process for enforcing the rules, as mandated by Civil Code and your governing documents, and the board needs to follow those procedures. (We will go into this in more detail in the chapter "How to Communicate with the Board.") An association can't simply fine a homeowner for a violation. Civil Code dictates that before a monetary penalty is imposed, the homeowner needs to be called to a hearing with the board of directors.

This is done to protect the homeowner. Before this requirement was in place, boards could impose a fine any time a violation happened. Notification was sketchy, if at all, and in some cases, the homeowners became aware of the infraction only after opening their statement and finding they owed hundreds of dollars.

This hearing is a chance for the homeowner to tell his or her side of the situation. This procedure can be inconvenient for both the homeowner and the association, but is worth it to make sure homeowners are aware of potential fines. Homeowners can respond to a hearing notice in writing, and that qualifies as appearing at the hearing.

Following the hearing, it is up to the board to review the evidence and determine whether or not a fine should be imposed.

Although an HOA board has many tasks, its main purpose is to make sure the business that is an HOA runs smoothly. From overseeing the finances to enforcing the rules, the board is there to protect and maintain your investment.

What Are the Duties of the Board?

When a person becomes a board member, he or she becomes your fiduciary. We've all heard the term "fiduciary duty," but what exactly does that mean? Fiduciary duty is a legal responsibility to act in another person's interest. It is the board member's job to take action on your behalf in regard to the HOA.

Being a fiduciary comes with certain responsibilities and expectations. The board is in place to maintain the property, enforce the rules, oversee the financial decisions of the HOA, and run the day-to-day operations. These decisions are made by a majority vote of the board. No one board member can make unilateral decisions unless it is an emergency situation or they are given the authority by the other board members. You expect the person who is representing you to act accordingly. She should be involved, informed, and interested.

Associations have lots of decisions that need to be made. Some decisions are major, like deciding on a painting contract that may cost over half a million dollars; others are small, like approving a plumber to fix a drain. Now imagine that you had to get a majority of your members to agree every time a decision needed to be made. A ballot would need to go out or a meeting scheduled, and 51% of your membership would need to attend to even be able to have the vote. If your association has one hundred homes, you would need fifty-one homeowners to appear before you could even begin to make decisions. This would be impractical, and nothing would get done.

So, the board of directors is appointed to make these decisions on your behalf. They don't have to vote the exact way you would, but they have the responsibility to make informed and educated decisions.

Board of Directors Meetings

In order to accomplish all this, board members need to participate in the process. This includes being responsive to management, educating themselves when needed, and making decisions in a timely fashion.

This is accomplished at board of directors meetings. There are two kinds of meetings for the board of directors—an open or general meeting and an executive session.

OPEN BOARD MEETING

HOA board of directors meetings fall under the Open Meeting Act. Under this law, the following requirements must be met in order to hold a meeting:

- Members are allowed to attend the meeting.
- At least four days' notice of the meeting has been given.
- An agenda has been posted.
- Members are given an opportunity to speak at the meeting.

Before attending an HOA meeting, it may be helpful to know what's expected of you and what you can expect.

Member Attendance

Even though the meeting is governed by the Open Meeting Act, that doesn't mean it is open to the general public. It is a homeowners association meeting, and membership in the organization—or, in the case of tenants, the approval of the association—is required for attendance. The purpose of a board meeting is for the board to conduct business. Since the decisions made by the board affect association members, they should, and have, a right to witness the process, and that is what the Open Meeting Act ensures.

Although your association adheres to the principles of the Open Meeting Act, that doesn't mean people can just walk in off the street and participate in your association's board meetings. Every once in a while, a non-community member will want to attend a meeting for some reason. This isn't very common, as most HOAs have a hard enough time getting their own members to attend, let alone anyone else.

In these cases where someone wanders in, the chair or management will simply ask them to leave.

Some associations will allow tenants to attend the board meetings, but this is not required, and it is a policy that the board needs to determine. In some cases, the number of rental units is so small that allowing the residents to attend isn't a problem. In other communities with a high rental population, having tenants at the meetings can become disruptive. A tenant may be allowed to attend but not to speak.

Sometimes tenants become very adamant about how the association should be operating and about services that should be provided but don't actually share in the costs. As an example, I was at a meeting where a tenant who was invited to attend the meeting demanded that cameras be added in strategic places around the complex. The board had already looked into this but found it to be very costly. This tenant rallied other residents, including homeowners, and forced the action. The cameras were installed, and each unit was assessed a special assessment to cover the cost. The tenant got the cameras she wanted, and the homeowners absorbed the cost of paying for them.

If renters or tenants are allowed to attend the meetings, it is recommended that the unit owner provide written notice authorizing the tenant to be there on their behalf. This safeguards the HOA should a dispute erupt between the tenant and the landlord. If a tenant continually interrupts or becomes disruptive at a meeting, the association has the right to bar them from future meetings.

Notice of the Meeting

A notice of when and where the board meeting is going to be held has to be posted at least four days prior to the meeting. The notice should be in a prominent location on the property and may be included in a newsletter, mailed, or distributed. Homeowners may request that notice of the meetings be mailed or emailed to them.

Agenda of the Meeting

The notice for the meeting should also include an agenda. The agenda should include topics that will be discussed. The board is permitted to take action only on items on the agenda. This allows homeowners to be aware of what is happening and reduces the risk of things being done behind their backs or in secret.

Sometimes things come up at the last minute and there isn't time to include them on the agenda or to give notice. Without proper notice, the item should be carried over to the next meeting, but this may not always be practical. In these cases, the board can motion to add these "unforeseen" items to the agenda, and provided the motion carries, the board can make a decision on them. These items should be few and should be items that the board became aware of after posting the meeting notice and agenda.

Here is a sample of a meeting agenda.

AGENDA

I.   CALL TO ORDER. This should note the location of the meeting, the establishment of a quorum, and the time of the meeting.

II. APPROVAL OF MEETING MINUTES. The minutes from the previous open session need to be approved by the board. Only open session minutes are approved here. Executive session minutes are approved in the executive session.

III. OPEN FORUM. This is the time for homeowners to say what is on their minds. The open forum is usually limited so the board will have time to tackle the issues they need to take action on. Some boards will move this forum to the end of the meeting in order for homeowners to observe the actions taken by the board before posing any concerns. The placement of the open forum is a board decision.

IV. TREASURER'S REPORT. This is where the financial statements are reviewed. These include the balances in each account, bank statements, income, expenses, and a comparison to the budget. Delinquencies may also be reviewed in this section. If a board is moving forward with filing a lien on a property, the motion to do so must be done in open session. The owner and account are referred to by the APN (Assessor Parcel Number) and not by name or address.

V.   MANAGER'S REPORT. This is where the management discusses any issues they may have. The manager may give a brief overview of the status of the community and any projects.

VI. COMMITTEE REPORTS. Committee chairs will either share a report with the board or provide a written report. If an action is needed or wanted by the committee, this is where they will make their case and get a response from the board.

VII. PRIOR BUSINESS. This line item always makes me laugh. When I started, it was called "Old Business." Then the meeting gods decided that sounded too informal, and it was changed to "Prior Business." But that was a bit too formal and confusing for some reason, and they went to "Unfinished Business." Now, as tends to happen, it is going back to "Old Business." Any of these titles is OK. This section is for any agenda item that was discussed at a previous meeting. This can be items that were tabled or just items that couldn't be completed in the time between meetings.

VIII. NEW BUSINESS. This is the place for any business that wasn't previously addressed at a board meeting. When issues come up that the board needs to address, they are added to this category. If a topic can't be completed or is tabled, it is added (or carried over) to the next meeting's agenda under Prior Business. It's important to stress that topics cannot be added here at the meeting unless voted on by the board, as stated above. If a topic that needs board action is broached at the meeting but isn't on the current agenda, it should be added to the next meeting's agenda. Even New Business items have to be noticed to homeowners.

IX. EXECUTIVE SESSION SUMMARY. Boards may meet in executive session to discuss certain issues, but they must note in the next general session that an executive session was held and the topics discussed.

X. ADJOURNMENT. Phew! The meeting is over and everyone can go home . . . unless there is an executive session, in which case the board and management have to stay. But this is the end of the general session. The date of the next meeting should be included if it has been determined.

Allowing a Member the Opportunity to Speak

Meetings are the only place where board members can make decisions. It is the arena for them to run the HOA business. They have to be allowed to discuss matters, exchange information, and make formal votes. Homeowners are allowed to witness this but not participate in the process. In order to give homeowners a chance to voice their opinions, every meeting must include a session for homeowners to speak. This is usually called "Open Forum" or "Homeowners' Forum."

As a homeowner, this is your time to say whatever you want. You can address issues on the agenda, procedures, or projects you would like to see in your neighborhood. Usually, thirty minutes is allotted for the open forum, although in some cases, this may be extended, and each homeowner is allowed three minutes to air their grievances. This is to allow time for everyone to speak. The chair does have the authority to allow someone extra time to address the board if the chair feels it is warranted.

Although you may bring up anything you like during the forum, the board is not required to take actions or respond to your items. In fact, if it's not on the agenda, the only action the board can take is to schedule the topic on a future agenda.

EXECUTIVE SESSION

Even though the board meetings are covered by the Open Meeting Act, the board is allowed to convene into executive sessions to discuss limited issues. Items that are handled in executive session include legal matters, formation of contracts (with the final approval of a contract being approved or ratified in open session), member discipline, delinquencies, and personnel. A homeowner may also request a meeting with the board in executive session to discuss issues of a sensitive nature.

Executive sessions are privileged. Those in attendance are not permitted to divulge information gleaned from these sessions unless they are authorized by the board to do so. Homeowners and prospective owners are not entitled to copies of the executive minutes, nor should these minutes be posted. The only time executive session minutes should be given out is as part of discovery in a lawsuit or if a subpoena is issued for the minutes.

The reason for executive sessions is not to allow the board to take action in secrecy. It is to allow the board to speak freely about sensitive issues without repercussions.

Meeting Decorum

A level of decorum needs to be established in order for the board to get work accomplished. This applies to both board members and homeowners. Some boards implement a code of conduct policy for the meetings. With or without this policy, here are some guidelines that should be followed.

For the board:

- **Establish a chairperson.** This may be the president, the manager, or anyone else the board decides on. The chair is the person who is going to run the meeting and should be determined prior to the meeting. The chair is the person who moves the meeting along, calls on others to speak— both board members and members of the audience—calls for votes when a formal vote is needed, and adjourns the meeting.

- **Follow or adopt *Robert's Rules of Order*.** OK, it doesn't have to be *Robert's Rules of Order*; it can be any form of parliamentary procedure. But an established protocol should be in place and used for the board meetings. Meetings don't have to be a formally run operation, but there should be a standard procedure that is made known to and followed by all in attendance.

- **Speak only when called upon.** The chairperson will call on people when it is appropriate for them to speak. Side conversations can be disruptive. If the chair has to continually repeat items, the meeting will go longer than necessary and some items may not be addressed in a timely fashion. Along this line is the common courtesy of not talking or texting on your cell phone during the meeting.

- **Participate in the meeting.** Be attentive during the duration of the meeting and participate when needed. When a vote is needed, be sure to cast a vote, either yes, no, or abstain. It's important to remember that all "no" votes must be verbalized. Remaining silent is not a negative vote.

- **Be passionate about your views, but know when to let go.** Every board member has an opinion, and every opinion should be heard. You should be passionate about your views, but be willing to let them go if you are in the minority.

- **Treat each other with respect.** You can disagree, even adamantly, but there should always be a level of respect. Every board member should treat the other members the way they want to be treated. Personal and petty arguments have no place in the board room.

- **Keep a sense of humor.** No matter what, remember this is only an HOA meeting. The business of the HOA is important, but it's not life threatening. Keep that in perspective.

For the homeowners:

- **Respect the procedure.** Although as a homeowner you are welcome to watch the meeting, you don't have a right to participate unless asked to do so by the chair. You will have the opportunity to ask questions during the open forum. Avoid interrupting the procedures with questions. If you are asked to sign in, sign in. If you need to fill out a card to speak during the open forum, please do so. The procedures are in place to facilitate the meeting and allow the board to cover as much as possible.

- **Keep side conversations to a minimum.** The board has to get work accomplished, and this can be difficult to do if the homeowners in attendance are having their own meetings. If you have to have a discussion with someone, step outside. It will allow you to talk about what you need to without stopping the meeting. This also goes for cell phones.

- **Be respectful.** Just as the board needs to be respectful, so should the homeowners. Be courteous to one another, to the board, and to any contractors at the meeting.

- **Try not to bring up individual, sensitive matters during the open forum.** Items like disciplinary action and delinquencies should be addressed in executive session.

Boards have a responsibility to act on your behalf in dealing with finances, personnel, individual issues, and all other aspects of running the association's business. Respecting and following the established protocol, although not always easy, allows the board to do their job. Knowing what is expected of a board can help you determine if your board is doing its job and to appreciate all that it does for you.

Good Board, Bad Board

I've worked with hundreds of different boards. Most have been honest, hardworking, decent, and effective, while others have been none of those things.

A good board is usually pretty easy to spot. When you look around the community, you see things are being accomplished. Routine maintenance is being done on schedule, and larger projects aren't just being talked about.

Don't laugh, but there is one surefire way to determine if your board is doing a good job: go to a board meeting. Look around. If there aren't any homeowners there, chances are high that your board is doing a pretty darn good job.

Some people will disagree with me and say, "No, homeowners aren't there because they are unhappy with the board." In my experience, this isn't the case. When people are upset about something, they turn out in droves. They want to air their concerns and make their voices heard. When things are going along smoothly, people stay home.

So, if you're on a board and no one is showing up to your meetings . . . congratulations, you most likely are doing a great job.

A good board is usually made up of good board members. A good candidate for the board is someone who puts the interest of the HOA above their own individual agenda. They take an interest in all aspects of the community, are willing to devote their time, and do what needs to be done. And believe it or not, homeowners who meet these qualifications aren't hard to find. These people make up good boards.

Warning Signs

But there are times when boards begin to falter, and this can affect your community. Here are some signs that may mean your board is in trouble:

BOARD MEMBERS SEEM MORE INTERESTED IN THEIR OWN INDIVIDUAL UNITS.

It's not unusual to take an interest in a cause that affects you, but as a board member, you have to be willing to put aside your own feelings and do what's best for the community as a whole.

One of my associations had a homeowner who was voted onto the board. At her first meeting, she brought up the issue of redoing the skylights in the community. The skylights were the responsibility of the individual homeowners, but she felt this was wrong. At every meeting, she would bring up this topic and present proposals from roofers who were willing to replace these skylights. She was insistent and would take over the meetings to present her viewpoint. Finally, the board gave in and agreed to redo the skylights. Her skylight was one of the first to be replaced. On the day her work was completed, she resigned from the board and put her unit on the market. It became apparent that the only reason she was on the board was to improve her unit to get a better selling price.

CANCELING OR NOT HAVING REGULAR BOARD MEETINGS.

Your governing documents will usually dictate how often your board should meet. Monthly is the norm, although bimonthly and quarterly are not unheard of. If your board starts changing the pattern of their meetings without explanation, this may be a red flag.

One association, in the midst of several lawsuits stemming from the Northridge earthquake, would meet on a weekly basis. This went on for about a year. Many homeowners took this as a sign that the board was inefficient. In reality, just the opposite was true. Some months, the board was asked to read over 400 pages of legal reports and documents and then make a decision. The board members knew they couldn't possibly do this in one two-hour session *and* accomplish all the things that needed to be done to keep the HOA afloat, so they gave up their time to get things done. That's dedication. A more common problem, though, is a board not having enough or having irregular meetings.

Along the same lines, monitor to see if your board cancels meetings at the last minute or routinely can't make quorum. Quorum is the minimum number of board members that are needed to hold the meeting. If board members aren't showing up, the association can't take care of business.

Occasionally a board may have to cancel a meeting. Board members are out of town, get sick, or get tied up at work. That's understandable. But if this continues on a regular basis, it becomes a problem. Some boards are so unreliable that when they ask me to attend their meetings, I put the date on the calendar in pencil.

Canceling meetings or not making quorum can have a financial impact as well. In some cases, management, room rentals, and vendors will get paid whether you have a meeting or not. In my case, as a recording secretary, I will be paid my minimum rate even if the meeting is cancelled due to a lack of a quorum.

PROCEDURE FOR MEETINGS IS NOT BEING FOLLOWED.

In the previous chapter, we discussed how a meeting should be run. There's an order that should be followed. If the board meetings don't follow the standard formula, that's an indication that something may be wrong.

It's not unusual for a board to add some items to the agenda. These are things that came up at the last minute and couldn't be on the posted agenda. It's not in the best interest of the HOA to hold them over for another month. (Remember the board can only take action at a board meeting.) In these cases, a motion is made to add the items to the agenda and, if approved, the board can discuss and vote on these issues.

It's OK to add two or three items at the last minute. More than that is an indication that work may not be getting done outside of the meeting or only being handled right before a meeting without sufficient time to get it completed. This may be due to trouble with the board and/or the management company. Either way, it is something to keep an eye on to make sure it doesn't develop into a pattern.

On occasion, the board never gets past the open forum. Owners are so disgruntled that the meeting quickly gets out of hand and the only way to regain order is to adjourn. Once this happens, no further items can be discussed, and everything gets delayed another month or until another night when the board is available and the meeting is reconvened. The board can move into executive session but can only address matters suitable for executive session.

DECISIONS ARE BEING MADE OUTSIDE OF A MEETING.

If work is being done, contracts entered into, or vendors being terminated without documentation in the minutes, this may be a sign that something is wrong. Civil Code allows for some decisions to be made outside of a board meeting, but it has to be classified as an emergency situation. An emergency would be something that affects the safety or well-being of the community (e.g., diseased tree that is at risk of falling) or a situation that needs attention, was unknown at the prior meeting, or could result in additional costs if work is delayed until the next meeting (e.g., roof leaks). All other things need to be discussed and decided at an open meeting. In addition, any decision made outside of a meeting, even in an emergency, needs to be documented in the next set of open session minutes so there is always a paper trail. If it appears this isn't being done, you may want to question the board.

WORK SEEMS TO BE AT A STANDSTILL.

You look around your community, and nothing is getting done. No work is underway. It feels like everything is deteriorating. The neighborhood is taking on a shabby appearance, and projects that were previously discussed seem to have stalled. This can be an indication that there are other issues consuming the board's attention or the board is in such discord that decisions can't be made.

ENFORCEMENT OF THE RULES IS NONEXISTENT.

When things start getting rough for an HOA, rule enforcement is one of the first things to go. It takes time for both management and the board to follow through on enforcement. When there are more pressing issues, enforcement tends to get lax.

If you begin to notice that people are doing whatever they want without any consequences, it is a sign that your board's attention may be elsewhere.

ATMOSPHERE AT THE MEETINGS IS HOSTILE.

Nothing is more unproductive than a board that spends it time bickering with one another or with the homeowners in attendance. Even though it is a volunteer board, there is no excuse for acting unprofessional.

LONGTIME VENDORS AND WORKERS DEPART.

There may be other reasons for a vendor to leave, but when you find multiple long-term vendors are leaving, there may be underlying reasons.

Sometimes a new board comes into power and decides to do a clean sweep of services. It's an almost "out with the old and in with the new"–type mentality. But this is usually a planned-out, orchestrated effort. The new vendors are lined up so there isn't downtime between the old and the new. But if you see vendors just walking off and no new service lined up, this may be an indication that something is wrong.

Recalling a Board

There are many reasons why a board may be displaying some of these warning signs. It can be that there are too many issues zapping productive time from your board and management. Is it one member who is causing a ruckus? There may be an ongoing lawsuit that is draining the association's resources. But it may be that you just don't have a cohesive board.

It may not be easy, but if you notice some of these signs, go to your board. Bring the topic up in open session and try to get some answers. It's a bit tricky because you are calling out a person or persons publicly. It may be necessary but should be approached with compassion.

Monitor the situation and try to determine what steps can be taken to turn things around. If it is one board member causing a problem, then, as homeowners, you may be able to put some pressure on him or her to resign. If there are extenuating circumstances that are creating a problem, you and other homeowners may be able to volunteer your time to try to get over the hump.

Even if the trouble is the overall board, there are steps you can take to improve the situation. For example, homeowners can take action to recall the entire board or select members.

In order to recall the board, you will need to do the following:

1. Draft a petition requesting a special meeting, where the sole purpose of this meeting is recalling the board (or individual members) and holding an election if the recall is successful.

2. Gather members' signatures on the ballot. 5% of the membership is required to proceed with the meeting.

3. Present the petition to the association. Once you obtain the required number of signatures on the petition, you need to give the petition to the HOA. Consult your governing documents to determine the correct procedure, but usually giving it to the management is acceptable.

4. Once received, the signatures will be verified for eligibility. This means the persons signing the petition must be on title and in good standing with the HOA. Tenants, multiple persons from one unit, and members who have had their voting privileges suspended don't count towards the 5% limit.

Once the petition is accepted and verified, the board is required to proceed with the special meeting to recall and vote in new board members if necessary. The HOA *must* schedule a date, secure a location, send out ballots (similar to the annual election), and properly notice the meeting.

You will need a quorum of the membership represented either with ballots or in person in order to open and count the ballots. Once the quorum is established, the meeting progresses like your annual election.

There are a few issues with recall elections. The HOA is required to absorb the costs for the special meeting and election, even if it is unsuccessful. Unless your governing documents state otherwise, there is no restriction barring recalled board members from nominating themselves to be on the ballot in the event that the recall goes through. This means you may go through this entire exercise and end up with the exact same board as when you started.

Even if you succeed and you end up with a new board, it is only in place until the regularly scheduled annual meeting. The replacement board only fills the remainder of the term of the board members they replaced. It may be more efficient and cost effective to wait until the next annual meeting and work on electing new members to the board at that time.

The process for replacing individual board members follows the same procedure. If you are seeking to replace just one or two members, it may be beneficial to have someone talk with them and ask for a resignation before going through this process. With a resignation, the remaining board members would vote in a replacement. This would save the association time and money. If they don't agree, you are no worse off.

It's not common, but every once in a while, you get a rogue board. If you find yourself in this predicament, don't panic. There are steps you can take to reverse the situation. If you have a good board in place, enjoy it . . . and be sure to thank the people who are making that happen.

How to Communicate with the Board

The board is made up of your representatives, who are there to make decisions for you and in your best interest. In one sense, they work for you, but in another, they are homeowners who have the right to enjoy their homes and families without being disturbed 24/7.

There are times when you will need to, and should be able to, communicate with your board. So how do you go about doing that?

Find out the most efficient way to reach your board. It may be through the management, or individual email addresses exclusively for board members (which some HOAs have), or the best method may be going to the board meetings and broaching the matter in the open forum. If you don't know, ask. Call your management company and tell them you would like to discuss a matter with the board and ask what method is preferred.

For some issues like maintenance, you don't really need to contact the board at all. These items are handled by the management anyway, and alerting them to the situation may be enough to get the job done. It may also be a quicker way to get work done.

If you have a topic of a sensitive nature that you would like to discuss, call the management company and request permission to discuss an issue with the board in executive session. This may include delinquencies, neighbor-to-neighbor disputes, violations, and personnel. If you are unable to attend the executive session, ask if a board member would be willing to meet with you privately. The board member is unable to make a decision at this meeting, but he or she can listen to you and take the matter back to the board to address. The meeting may also provide you with some guidance to address your concern.

There are two ways you can reach out to your board members: in person, by attending a meeting, or through written communication like a letter or email.

Attending a Board Meeting

As I've mentioned, there is always an open forum at the board meeting, and you can bring up topics. Items in the open forum aren't immediately added to the agenda, but it may be something the board can discuss at a future meeting. (See the previous chapter for more information on the agenda process.) Even though the board may not be able to address your issue on the spot, it can steer you in the right direction in order to resolve the matter. More important, it is an opportunity to make the board aware of conditions that you have concerns about.

Written Letter

There's always the old-fashioned method of sending a letter. Be sure to send the letter to the management office, which may not be the same place you send your monthly assessments. Often payments go directly to a lock box, and they aren't equipped to deal with correspondence. Including correspondence with your payment can cause a delay in getting your letter to the right person.

Of course, you may email your board members at their designated addresses or through management. The same rules apply for electronic communications.

Any written communication addressed to the board—either by email or snail mail—that is sent to management must be given to the board, even if it is something negative.

Tips for Contacting the Board

No matter which method you choose, there are some things to keep in mind when contacting the board.

- **Respect a board member's personal life.** Volunteering on a board doesn't mean you give up the right to quiet, peaceful enjoyment of your home.

Association business shouldn't be discussed on a board member's front lawn, at baseball practice, in the grocery store, or in the workplace. Go through the proper channels.

- **Never call a board member at home or work unless invited to do so.** Some directors have no problem with this and give out their number to anyone who asks. But if they don't, respect their right to privacy.

- **Don't resort to name-calling.** Whether it's to the board members, neighbors, management, or vendors, avoid the urge to use any demeaning names. I'm always surprised when I see adults who should know better sink to this level. You may have a valid concern or complaint, but this tactic diminishes your argument.

- **Be polite and courteous.** You don't have to agree, but you do have to be neighbors. Treat all board members the way you yourself would want to be treated.

Responding to a Violation Letter

One of the most common reasons and the biggest bones of contention for contacting a board member is a violation letter. Understanding the process for sending and receiving violation letters may help to reduce the stress in this process.

Every association has a different violation and fine schedule, so be sure to check your governing documents for the one that applies to your home. If a violation is levied against you, here is an idea of what to expect.

RECEIVING THE VIOLATION

A violation can be reported in different ways. A neighbor may make a complaint, management may spot the violation on a site visit, security may report it, or in some cases the association hires a third party to come through and do enforcement. Once a violation is received, notification is sent to you. This brings to your attention that there is something wrong and you need to make a correction. The letter will usually give you a certain amount of time to make the necessary fix.

If, for some reason, you don't make the repair or the violation reoccurs, then a hearing or a Notice of Intent to Fine letter is sent. This is a more serious letter. It tells you that the HOA may impose a fine and is asking you to appear before the board to address the issue. The fine letter must include certain information: the alleged violation; the amount of the proposed fine; and the date, time, and place where the hearing will take place.

If you get a hearing letter, do not ignore it, even if you corrected the violation. Call the management company and let it know that you took care of the issue and ask if you should attend the hearing. Don't assume someone will inspect your property before the scheduled meeting date. Most boards will look at no response as an admission of guilt and assess the fine.

ATTENDING A HEARING

With a Notice of Intent to Fine letter, you have two options. One is to attend the hearing, and the other is to submit a response in writing. It's important to note that a written response does constitute an appearance at the hearing. In lieu of you being there, the board will review your response and make its decision.

You may want to attend the hearing and present your case to the board. This meeting with the board isn't meant to be, nor should it be, confrontational. The purpose of the hearing is to give you an opportunity to be heard and for the board to get all the facts. You may have a reason for why something wasn't done or simply be unaware that what you did was a violation. This is your chance to present your side of the story.

Avoid coming to the hearing with a chip on your shoulder. And in all honesty, the board shouldn't have a chip on its shoulder either. You should treat the board members with respect, and they should treat you with respect. If you committed the violation, and we all do at one time or another, own up to it. Say you're sorry and that it won't happen again. If you disagree with the rule, let the board know. You may still need to make the correction, but the board may be able to advise you how to go about changing the rule. If you need additional time to make the correction, this is the time to ask the board for that consideration.

Some homeowners will bring their attorney with them to these hearings. You have the right to do so, but usually this isn't necessary. Bringing an attorney may escalate the situation.

THE BOARD'S DECISION

After you say your piece at the hearing, you will be asked to leave. The board will discuss the matter and make a determination. It can waive the fine, meaning the violation is removed as if it never happened. It can suspend the fine contingent upon certain conditions being met, most likely that there be no further violations. Technically the fine is imposed, but it is not assessed to your account at this time. It is held it in abeyance and will be added to your account only if the terms aren't met. Or the board can impose the fine, and the amount is immediately added to your association account.

A letter stating the board's decision will be sent to you within fifteen days of the hearing. If you are unhappy with the board's decision or feel there is evidence that the board didn't consider, you can request an appeal. Draft an email or letter asking the board to reconsider the decision and ask that the matter be heard at the next executive session.

It is important to note that HOAs cannot foreclose on fines. An association can take a homeowner to small claims court for unpaid fines. If they win, they can foreclose on an unpaid judgment. Although associations may face limits on the actions they can take on uncollected fines, the fines will remain on your account and can prevent you from refinancing your unit or selling it. So fines should be taken care of in a timely fashion.

If you do get a violation letter, don't take it personally. This is a standard method of alerting you to something that needs your attention. It's not meant as a personal attack and is no reflection on you as a person, homeowner, or neighbor.

Communication is a vital part of a successful HOA. As a member of the association, you have the right to express your opinions, suggestions, and concerns to the board. Boards are anxious to hear what you have to say and appreciate your comments. But it does need to be done in a professional, friendly, and appropriate manner.

PART THREE

MANAGEMENT

What Is the Management?

Your HOA is a business run by a board of directors. These directors are homeowners or residents who have a vested interest in your community, but they are also volunteers who may have jobs, family, and commitments to take up their time. Running the HOA may be far down on their list of priorities.

That's not a criticism; it's the truth. Just like any other business, the HOA has everyday tasks that need to be done. Bills have to be paid, vendors contacted—vendors who work only during regular business hours—work scheduled, and communications drafted and sent. As discussed in the "Purpose of the Board" chapter, boards are typically prohibited from being paid for performing their duties, and it's hard to ask someone to give up his or her life for the sake of the HOA.

That's where a manager steps in. A manager or management company is an agent of the association hired by the board of directors to handle the everyday ins and outs of running the HOA's business. The HOA hires a landscape service because you wouldn't expect your board to spend its Saturdays mowing your lawns. (OK, there are some people who may expect that, but it's unrealistic.) The same is true for managing the affairs of the association, and that's where management comes in.

Managers are hired by associations to perform certain tasks. They are paid a monthly fee and are contracted to do specific jobs. In most cases, managers don't have a vote on the board, are not authorized to spend the HOA's funds, and cannot enter into contracts for service or goods. But they organize all those things so the board can take action as soon as it meets. In other words, they do the groundwork that the board most likely doesn't have the time to do.

Duties of the Management

As you are probably becoming aware, nothing in HOAs is cut and dry. There are exceptions to every rule, and that goes for management as well. In the previous paragraph, I told you things your manager couldn't do, and now I'm going to take some of it back.

Your manager acts at the direction of your board. Oftentimes the board will vote limited authorization to the manager in order to allow the business to run more efficiently. Your board may vote that your manager has the power to approve a proposal, provided the cost for services is under $500. The dollar limit is determined by a vote of the board. Everything is spelled out, documented, and predetermined.

This action allows small jobs to be completed quickly and without a board vote. For example, imagine that your pool man comes out and finds that the water pump is in need of repair. The cost is $248.76. Without this existing authorization in place, management would have to do an email vote of the board to approve the expenditure if the repair is deemed an emergency or wait until the next open board meeting to present it to the board for approval. Either way takes time and delays the maintenance of the property. With this approval in place, management can give the go-ahead for the fix and notify the board of the expenditure. But if the cost of repairs had been $501.00 or more, the manager wouldn't be able to approve it and the matter would have gone to the board for a yes or no.

The board may also authorize management to sign a contract for it. For example, the board may have gotten bids to paint the guardhouse. At the meeting, it is determined that two of the proposals are very similar, but one doesn't account for power washing before painting. The board believes it's included but isn't sure, so it directs management to get this information and authorize him or her to make a decision between the two proposals.

The manager would have to make the decision based on the board's prerequisites. He couldn't go out and hire a different vendor. He has the authority only to choose between the two. If the manager wanted to hire another painter, he would have to go back to the board for approval.

In either case, management is acting within the limits that the board has given it. Its actions are either spelled out in the signed management contract or allowed by a vote of the board.

Your manager also serves as the liaison between you and your board. As a homeowner, management is your first step when you have a question, a complaint, or a request. This can result in numerous calls, emails, or visits. Managers address what they can and pass along the necessary information to the board for action. Managers do the preliminary legwork for board members.

Some homeowners want to know why they can't simply contact the board themselves. The reason is that it's not unusual for a manager to walk into the office on a Monday morning and have fifty messages waiting for a response. Each one needs attention and action. It's the manager's job to follow up on these items.

Imagine if you went to work and first thing on a Monday morning, you were inundated with phone calls, texts, emails—all demanding your time and attention and not one of them having anything to do with the job you're getting paid for. Your boss wouldn't be too happy, and neither would the company employing your board members. That's the scenario that board members would face if there wasn't a manager or management company overseeing the HOA. Having the manager as the point person takes the burden off the board, and it allows board members to enjoy their homes and communities without having to constantly handle HOA business.

The Different Kinds of Management

No two HOAs are alike. The needs of your community are going to be different than those of the neighborhood down the street. To accommodate those varying needs, there are different kinds of management. You can be self-managed, independently managed, or have a management firm. Even within a management firm, there are different kinds of managers. Let's look at each one.

SELF-MANAGED

This is where the board of directors hires a manager from within the community. This person may be a homeowner or a tenant who takes on the paid responsibility of running your business. He or she either works from home or on the property if space is available.

One benefit to self-managing is that you have an employee who has a vested interest in your HOA. He or she knows the ins and outs and quirks of the association and usually has a good feel for what is going on with the homeowners.

There are drawbacks to this option, however. First, it can be pricey. You not only have to pay the salary of the person who is managing you, but you also become an employer. With current trends, that salary you will be paying will be a minimum of $15.00 an hour. There are legal ramifications, requirements, and insurance that go along with this option and need to be taken into consideration. The HOA will be responsible for insurance, taxes, and all requirements for having an employee. You may have to provide certain benefits or compensation for those benefits. The HOA is also responsible for providing the tools of the trade—paper, supplies, copies, postage, etc.

Another drawback is that the association will need a plan for emergencies, after-hour calls, and times when the manager is away. Even the most dedicated employee is unavailable at some time. The board may consider a message center or another person to have on call when the manager is away. These fill the HOA's needs, but they do come at a cost.

This option also gives one person in your community a lot of power. Yes, he or she is overseen by the board, but the manager has access to individual homeowners' financial information, personal information, and, in some cases, even their homes.

The HOA is at the hands of this person. His or her actions—intentionally or unintentionally—affect you. I worked with one HOA that had a homeowner manage the property on a part-time basis. It worked fine until her husband got transferred. She gave the board less than a week's notice to find her replacement. She had known for months but didn't say anything because she didn't want to lose the income. She left the HOA in a lurch and unmanaged for a short period of time.

People do get sick, have family crises, and simply get burnt out. Any self-managed property should have a contingency plan at the ready in the event the HOA and the manager part ways.

I have to admit that I have worked for a few self-managed properties and I have never seen it work successfully long term. Managers have to make tough and unpopular decisions. That's not an easy thing to do, and it gets even harder when the person you're saying no to is your neighbor.

I worked at one property that was managed full time by a homeowner. She was friendly with the board, and they went for drinks every Friday night—that is, until she had a falling out with her friend who was on the board. The fight had nothing to do with the HOA, but it quickly carried over into the everyday operations. In fact, when I went to the meetings, it was my job to sit between the two to keep them separated. The business suffered, the manager was fired, the board member involved sold her unit (she said she couldn't live in the midst of such conflict even though she had a hand in creating it), and outside management was quickly hired.

I'm sure there are some associations that are successfully self-managed, but it does take a lot of work.

INDEPENDENTLY MANAGED

This is where an individual—either as an independent contractor, a sole proprietor, or a small corporation—takes on the management of your HOA. He or she may have an assistant, but generally it is a one-person operation. This person isn't an employee of the association, but rather, the association is one of his or her clients.

The advantage of this type of manager is that you get what you see: the person presented to the HOA is the one who will be managing it. During the interview process, you should get an idea of how this person conducts himself or herself. Does he or she return phone calls? Is he or she knowledgeable of the business? Does he or she have a good understanding of your complex?

Another benefit of this manager is that you are his or her bread and butter. He or she has to do a good job to keep your business and keep that income coming in. An employee of a larger company has the ability to push you off to another employee. The independent manager can't do that without losing revenue.

The drawbacks of an independent manager are similar to those of a self-manager. You are bound by this person's limitations. If the independent manager goes on an extended vacation, you are basically without management for that duration. If he or she gets sick, you have to slow down or shut down.

I worked for years with a wonderful independent manager. She limited the number of accounts she took on and worked diligently for her customers. Then one day, I showed up at the board meeting and she was waiting for me outside. (It's never a good sign when someone wants to talk to you privately before or after a meeting.) She said, "I want you to know I won't be here next month." I thought she was going on vacation, which was sort of true. She announced at the meeting that she was going into immediate retirement and the HOA had two weeks to find other management. It turned out she had some personal issues that needed attention, and she was closing up shop. The board had to vote in new management fast, and it took the HOA a while to recover.

Even with the potential drawbacks, an independent manager is usually a very dedicated worker. This person is able to pick and choose his or her clients. The independent manager wants your business and is willing to work to keep it.

MANAGEMENT FIRM

This is probably the most common way to manage an HOA. A management company can be large or small. It can have hundreds of employees or just a handful. But you aren't hiring a specific manager; you hire the company.

Some of the benefits of a management firm are that you get a team of people working on your account. Where the self- and independent managers have to farm out a lot of their everyday tasks, the larger companies handle all those things in-house. In addition to property managers, they usually have an accounting department, escrow division, customer service, assistants, and upper management.

No matter what happens, it is the job of the management company to continue to manage your property. Going with a management firm doesn't eliminate the issues you have with an individual manager, but there is a support network in place to pick up any loose pieces. If your manager quits, the company needs to find a replacement. If your manager is on vacation, there is someone there to continue to oversee your property.

Even within a management company, there are two different kinds of managers.

Dedicated Manager: This is a manager who has only one HOA to oversee. If it is a larger property, this may be a full-time position. If you are a smaller association, then the manager may only work a few days a week or a few hours a day, but those hours are dedicated to only your association. A dedicated manager may work on-site at the property or out of the corporate office.

Portfolio Manager: This is more typical of a manager who works in a management company. The portfolio manager has a number of properties that he or she manages. The employee may work eight hours a day, but only a portion of that time is for your association. Usually this manager works out of the corporate office and visits the property as needed or required by the contract. The benefit of a portfolio manager is that it usually is less expensive for the association. If you have a dedicated manager, then your costs must cover his salary as well as overhead for the company. When you share an employee with other HOAs, you also share the overhead.

There are a few factors your HOA should consider when engaging a management company. The cream of the crop would be to have a full-time manager with your HOA as his or her sole client. You have the manager's undivided attention for eight hours a day. Of course, this is the most expensive option and usually not viable for many associations. This is usually only an option for larger associations that have more assessments coming in and therefore more funds available. If costs are a concern, your board will look at other, more cost-effective options.

The board will need to evaluate the needs of your HOA and select the best method of management for your group. I've worked with all of the above managers, and there really isn't one that is better than the others. I've seen each of these methods succeed beautifully, and I've seen them fail miserably.

When deciding what kind of management company to go with, the key is to be honest about the needs of the community. If an HOA has a lot of issues going on—deferred maintenance, legal battles, difficult homeowners—then a part-time, independent manager may not be the best choice. A dedicated manager may be ideal, but not if homeowners can't afford the assessments needed to cover the higher costs. If the board and homeowners like the hands-off approach, then you may want to go with a full-service firm.

As a homeowner, you aren't involved in the actual hiring of the manager, as that is done by the board, but even if you aren't included in the decision-making process, it's important to know what kind of manager you have. This way, you will be aware of the level of service you can and should expect.

What Should I Expect from Management?

Every once in a while, homeowners will call their management company just to let them know they are doing a good job. It's not unheard of, but unfortunately, it's not very common. Property management is a complaint-driven profession. More often, managers receive a homeowner calling with a grievance, a problem, or a concern.

These calls can escalate quickly. The homeowner has a problem and wants it taken care of. The manager may be working on it, but we all know that when it comes to our own individual problems, fast is simply not fast enough. We get frustrated. And when it comes to dealing with a property manager, the usual retort is "I pay you X amount of dollars each month; do your job!"

Without going into who is right and who is wrong (that's not something we can deal with here without details), let's look at that statement. Many homeowners think that the management company gets the assessment they pay every month because the check is sent to the management company. But that is not the case.

To understand this a little better, let's take a look at a monthly assessment from one of my accounts. There are 240 condo units in this association, and each unit pays a monthly assessment of $324.00. So each month, the homeowner in our example writes a check to her association—not the management company. She sends it to the management company, but it is deposited into the association's operating account.

The association must pay its bills from that $324.00. Here is the breakdown of what each individual at that HOA pays on a monthly basis:

Insurance (Earthquake and Liability)	$41.70
Taxes (Preparing and Payment)	$ 1.70
Utilities (Gas, electric, water etc.)	$81.50
Landscaping	$44.45
Pool	$ 3.70
Pest Control	$ 2.60
Repairs/Maintenance	$40.50
Security	$ 3.10
Reserve Deposit	$86.80
Administrative (Printing, postage)	$ 4.20

That leaves a whopping $13.75 for your management company. That means that out of the $324.00 each homeowner pays, the management company is only "keeping" $13.75 . . . a month.

Now that we have the numbers (of course, yours will be different, but you can easily figure out what portion of your assessment is going toward the different elements by requesting a copy of your annual budget), we can fill in the number on our previous exclamation:

"I pay you $13.75 a month; do your job!" Just doesn't quite have the same bite, does it?

Please understand that this exercise isn't meant to make excuses for management. Once the management company or manager accepts your association's money, he or she is expected to perform certain tasks. But rather, this exercise is meant to put into perspective the amount your manager is actually getting paid.

Reasonable Expectations

Here are some things you should expect from your management company for the fees you are paying:

ACCESSIBILITY TO HOMEOWNERS.

The management company is the go-between for you and your board. As we talked about earlier, not many people would volunteer to serve on a board if they were required to take homeowners' phone calls 24/7. That's why you pay management the $13.75. It handles the calls and emergencies and runs the business for you. If you can't reach it, the system falls apart and things don't get done.

With that said, you shouldn't expect your manager to sit by the phone just waiting for you to call. Managers have a lot on their plates. They are dealing with other clients, multiple homeowners, vendors, and board members. You do need to have some patience and allow them a reasonable amount of time to get back to you. It's always a good idea to find out from your manager what method of communication he prefers. Some would like you to email them; others want a phone call. Use whatever method will get you the quickest response.

Most management companies will have an emergency line for after-hour situations. If a call comes in, the manager will be contacted at home to handle the situation. Be mindful of what situations constitute an emergency and what can wait until normal business hours. An emergency is if property is being damaged or people are in danger. A broken pipe spewing water is an emergency. Wondering whether or not you paid your dues isn't.

I once assisted at a management company and was working the Fourth of July weekend when a homeowner called to request that his name in the electronic directory at the gate be changed. Apparently he was having a party and, for some unknown reason, gave the guests a different name than what was listed in the entrance directory. Therefore, he wanted another name added so his guests would be able to look him up and he could buzz them in. To him, this was an emergency, but in reality, it was just bad planning. He was told that the company that makes those changes was closed for the holiday, and it would be scheduled after the weekend. He became incensed and yelled that it would be done by the end of the day or else. He then proceeded to call the emergency line every fifteen minutes demanding that this be done. The calls continued until 2:00 a.m. when the person handling the emergency line couldn't take it any longer. And no, the name in the directory didn't get changed. Instead, the homeowner received a call from the management's and association's attorney telling him to stop . . . or else.

RESPECT TOWARDS HOMEOWNERS.

Homeowners should feel comfortable contacting the management office. Their requests should be answered in a courteous and polite manner. That doesn't mean all requests will be honored, because managers are limited in what they can and can't do. Some actions require board approval, and often that can't be obtained until a board meeting. That should be explained to the homeowner and then followed up on.

On a related note, at no point should your management use crude or vulgar language. I would love to say that this has never happened with any of the managers I've worked with, but that isn't true. Frustration sometimes gets the best of us, but that's no excuse. You are the client, and you should be treated with respect.

FULFILLMENT OF REQUESTS.

Yes, there are things that need board approval and can't be acted upon immediately, but that doesn't mean they should be forgotten. If for some reason your request can't be completed immediately, management should explain this to you. To receive a follow-up phone call or email is not an unreasonable expectation for a homeowner.

KNOWLEDGEABILITY.

A good manager will know the business. Property management is a fluid field. The rules, codes, and laws are constantly changing, and good managers are aware of these changes. They know the ins and outs of all aspects of the business and are willing to share that expertise with homeowners who may not be as familiar with the industry as they are. Of course, no one person is expected to know everything all the time. But your manager should have the resources to find out quickly.

Your manager should also be knowledgeable about your specific HOA and familiar with the governing documents, properties, vendors, and procedures.

TAKING CARE OF BUSINESS.

This one seems like it should be a given. After all, that's what you're paying management for. Things should be getting done. The wheels of property management tend to turn slowly, and you do have to be aware of that. But at any given point, a manager should be able to give you an overview of what has been done and a status update on projects.

Now that you have an understanding about what management is and what you should expect from it, how do you go about hiring the best company or person for your property?

Hiring Management

The hiring of management is the responsibility of the board. But as a homeowner, it is a good idea to be familiar with the procedure and what goes into that final decision.

Board members often ask me to recommend a good management company. I hesitate to do so for a few reasons, but mainly because you can have a really good manager who works for a not-so-great company and vice versa.

I liken picking a manager/management company to dating. You want to select not only a candidate whom you like but also one who is going to have staying power.

Some HOAs will form a committee to vet managers. If you are on a board or committee saddled with this task, here is some advice to get through the process.

INTERVIEW THE MANAGEMENT COMPANY.

When selecting a manager, the first thing you should do is interview the company. Schedule a meeting with the head honchos and meet at your property. No matter how many other properties a manager may manage, your property is different. Walk the area. We all look good on paper, but visiting the property gives the management company a realistic view of what it may be undertaking.

One manager learned this the hard way. I recommended him for a property, and he presented a proposal and was quickly hired. After a month, I asked him how it was going. He said, "Man, I should have visited this property before signing the contract because I would have doubled my fee."

You don't want to go through the whole process, select a firm, and sign a contract only to find out that the manager has either underbid the property or is in over his head. Be upfront. Talk about your concerns, your plans for the property, and what you would like to see. Also bring up any problems you may be experiencing. If you have a large amount of delinquent accounts, let the prospective manager know. If you are facing major construction, let him or her know.

The more information on your property the management team has, the better it will be able to serve the needs of your community.

VISIT THE OFFICE.

Just as important as it is for the management team to see your property, it is also important for you to visit its location. Stop by the office. Is it professional, friendly, easy for homeowners to get to if needed?

I worked briefly with one management company and went to its offices to drop off papers. The office building was in a very congested part of town, and parking was nonexistent. The only option was to valet park. I was just dropping something off, so I figured it wouldn't be too bad. That fifteen-minute visit cost me twenty bucks. This is definitely something you would want to know before entering into an agreement. You want to make sure your manager's office is not only professional but also convenient for homeowners, board members, and vendors to visit if necessary.

CALL THE OFFICE.

Call the office. Do you get a nice reception? Does the company handle phone calls in a professional and friendly manner? Remember that the management firm is the first impression for anyone who contacts your association, and it should be a good one. Be sure it presents the image you want. During the interviewing process, be sure to call at some point and leave a message for your contact person. Does he or she call back quickly? Did he or she have the answers you wanted? This is the wooing period, so if the company isn't treating you right here, it's probably not going to get better.

INTERVIEW *YOUR* MANAGER.

When you're ready to hire a manager, you've moved from dating to marriage—

you're going to be spending a lot of time with this person, so you better make sure you like them. Interview not only the company but also the actual person who will be managing your account. If the management firm is undecided on who that person will be, put in the contract that you have the right to approve the manager.

Working with a manager is a relationship, and you have to be sure you like and trust that person. We've all had a date—some of us more than we care to admit—where half a glass of wine into it, we know it'll never work and want it to be over. Now imagine being locked into a contract, forced to work with that person, and having him oversee the place where you live. It's not a good situation.

Your manager should have a personality that suits your community. If you have a laid-back, easygoing group, then a Type-A, driven person may not work for you. And vice versa. If you have a gung-ho, involved board that is always on the go, then a manager with a wait-and-see attitude may not be the best choice.

The candidate who is going to work at your complex should know the business and show initiative to learn *your* business. No two HOAs are the same, and there is going to be a learning curve any time you have a new manager. The new person will have to learn your policies, your likes and dislikes. The manager will have to learn the ins and outs of your property and the little quirks that we all have.

It sounds like we're talking about dating again, but it's true. Your manager will need time to get acquainted and adjusted. Not having all the answers at the beginning is not a problem, but not having the initiative or enthusiasm to find out the answers is.

Often, it's easy to spot if a manager is right for your property. I went to a meeting one night with a new manager. It was her third meeting . . . OK, her second meeting, because she called in sick to one of the earlier meetings—not a good sign in and of itself. During the board meeting, she spent the majority of the time texting on her phone. When asked a question, she would respond, "I don't know. I'll have to find out and get back to you." After the meeting, one of the board members walked me to my car and asked what I thought of the new manager. I wasn't impressed and was having trouble finding a diplomatic way to say so. As I was hemming and hawing, the board member saved me by saying, "I know. I think the same thing."

This association had many ongoing issues that needed immediate attention. It was clear this manager didn't have the skills or desire to meet the challenges of this HOA, and a replacement manager was requested. This isn't to say the manager is bad or should have been fired, but she wasn't right for *that* property.

As a board member or homeowner, you should be able to voice any concerns you have with the management to the management, provided it is done in a respectful manner. Earlier we said that management should treat you with respect, and that is a two-way street.

If you have legitimate issues with management, you should be able to discuss them with the company freely. Ask to talk to a manager and let him or her know that the intent of your discussion is to improve service. Management will be working together with the members of your association, and for both your sakes, you want that relationship to be comfortable and productive.

You, your board, and your management all have the same goal: to make your association run efficiently and as effortlessly as possible. Working together as a team is the best way to make that happen.

What Happens If Management Isn't Doing Its Job?

Management is a big cog in the wheel that keeps your HOA churning. It is the liaison between you and your board and between your board and vendors, and it is the facilitator for the everyday operations of your association. So what happens when that vital team member falls down on the job?

As a homeowner, it can be frustrating when you feel management isn't doing what it is being paid to do, because you don't have a voice in hiring or retaining them. This responsibility lies directly with the board. The board may listen to the homeowner's complaints, but ultimately the decision of whether to keep the management or make some kind of change is up to the board.

The unfortunate part is that whenever something goes wrong, management usually gets the blame whether it deserves it or not. If you get a violation, it's because of management. If your project isn't approved, it's because of management. If repairs aren't being completed quickly, it's management's fault. A lot of times, though, management is simply the scapegoat. The manager doesn't live in the community, and it's easier to take out our frustrations on him.

Let me share a story that just happened to me. A homeowner called because of a water leak in her unit. She contacted me because she felt management wasn't doing enough to complete the work in her condo and thought I could help. She said that management had promised the contractor would be out on Tuesday to begin work. It was Friday, and they hadn't shown up. She ended with, "Can you believe they are treating me this way?"

I said, "Well, there are two sides to every story."

She responded, "No, there is only one, and it's my side."

So, of course, I called management and relayed the conversation. Yes, the manager had promised her they would start work on Tuesday, but when the workers showed up, her tenants refused to allow them access to the unit. The tenants told the crew to come back another day. The contractor and his team left and said they would come back when their schedule permitted.

Definitely a different story. And not the manager's fault.

It's also important to remember that management is limited in what it can and can't do. The board makes the decisions, and in a lot of cases, management is not authorized to act. This can cause delays and frustration.

As an example, let's look at getting architectural approval for a project. Some homeowners think they can walk their plans into the management office and get immediate approval. This normally isn't so. The plans need to be submitted to either a committee or the board to review and make a decision. The manager and his or her office staff don't have the power to approve your plans on the spot, and no amount of screaming or yelling will change that. There is a process that management has to follow.

Warning Signs

There are times, however, when management begins to slip. Whether you are a board member or homeowner, here are some warning signs to keep an eye out for.

COMING TO MEETINGS UNPREPARED.

To me, this is always a big red flag. If it happens once or twice, that's OK. Or if there is a lot going on in the community, it may be understandable that some of the smaller projects have taken a backseat. But if it becomes commonplace, it's an issue.

As your board works its way through the meeting agenda, see how many items are tabled. Remember a board meeting is the only place your board can make a decision. If, month after month, items are pushed back due to not having information, then management isn't doing something.

MANAGER IS UNINVOLVED.

Some managers begin to show a lack of enthusiasm. This can happen with newbies to your property but also with a manager who has been there for a while. He or she might begin to miss meetings with no reason or a weak excuse, cancel at the last minute, or be inattentive during meetings. As homeowners, you need a manager who is going to represent your best interests, and that means taking an interest in all aspects of your community.

PHONE CALLS AND HOMEOWNER REQUESTS ARE NOT BEING ANSWERED.

I joke and say I wish I were paid by the number of times a homeowner complains, "Management didn't return my call." This seems to be the catchphrase anytime something isn't done. Sometimes it's true—management really didn't return a homeowner's phone calls—and other times it's not. Unfortunately, this has become such a common and overused statement that it has lost a lot of its effectiveness. When a homeowner makes this claim, it is usually disregarded.

But just because it is used often doesn't mean management should use it as an excuse to avoid homeowners' phone calls, simply because it's easier for them. That's not acceptable.

If you feel your manager is ignoring you, keep a log. List when you call or email; whom you spoke with; if you didn't speak to a person, whom you left a message for; any action that was requested and/or promised; and the timeframe for completing the task. Be sure to log any follow-up action that is taken. Be honest. If the manager sent you an email, put it down. If the topic was added to the agenda for the board to discuss, mark that down, as that's an action. If you begin to notice a pattern of neglect, present your log to the board.

Keeping a log will also help you assess whether you are truly being ignored or just being impatient. Being impatient is OK and, in some cases, understandable. It's your home, and you want matters taken care of quickly. But there is a difference between things not getting done quickly and being slighted.

It's important that you as a homeowner have a reliable line of communication between you and your HOA, and it is the manager's job to be that point person.

BUSINESS IS NOT BEING DONE.

There are certain things that boards *have* to do, many of which the board is unaware of. Boards are fluid and may change from year to year. HOAs don't have professional boards, so many of the requirements are unknown to the members. It's the duty of management to remind the board what is needed of the individual board members.

As an example, one HOA didn't have an annual meeting for five years even though the governing documents required an election to be held every year. The manager just never got around to scheduling it. The board would ask, and the manager would say, "Oh, yeah, I'm sending out the nomination forms next month." And then nothing was done. A few months would go by and a board member or homeowner would ask, and it would be the same old song and dance. This was only one case of neglect by this manager. The board caught on and the manager was removed.

If management does bring something to the board's attention and the board chooses not to act on management's recommendations, then the fault may lie with your board and not management.

MISTAKES ARE BEING MADE.

OK, we all make mistakes. It's human nature. It becomes an issue when the mistakes are numerous and careless. Are you receiving communication for a different association? Are there typos and misinformation in your newsletter? Are letters being sent to the wrong person? Are invoices being paid incorrectly?

When it came time to do the budget, one association noticed that its utility bills had increased dramatically over the year and questioned this. Management said it was the cost of inflation and dismissed it. One board member in particular refused to let it go and continued to pursue it. It turned out the management company's accounting department was confusing two associations that had similar names, and this one was paying all the utility bills for both associations.

As we said, mistakes are inevitable. Your manager will make a boo-boo from time to time. The real consideration is how management handles an error when it's brought to its attention. Is it corrected quickly, courteously, and without cost to the HOA? In the example above, once the issue with the utility bills was brought to light, the management company immediately wrote a check to reimburse the association for the overpayment and remedied the situation with the utility company and the other HOA.

Mistakes happen, but are they happening more often than they should be? A mix-up every once in a while is understandable, but when it starts to become commonplace, that's trouble.

MANAGER CONTINUOUSLY SUPPLIES MISINFORMATION.

"Misinformation" sounds so much nicer than "lies," but that's really what it is. I'm not referring to the occasional wrong answer or momentary confusion. We all experience those now and again. I mean blatant, straight-out, intentional lies.

Usually this occurs when a manager needs to cover his or her own behind. The manager neglected to do something or did something incorrectly, and instead of owning up to it, he or she passes the blame on to someone else.

This is a big issue because you need to be able to trust your manager. He or she has access to vital information—your bank accounts, your personal identification information, your property. You may disagree with a manager's work style, but you have to have faith that your manager is doing the right thing and giving you accurate information.

One HOA lost faith in its manager when she was out of work for a week due to illness. It was unexpected and put a burden on not only the HOA but also the management company, which had to cover for her. Everyone was understanding because she was sick . . . that was, until the pictures of her vacationing in Mexico started appearing on Facebook.

PROJECTS ARE BEING DELAYED FOR NO REAL REASON.

There are a number of reasons why projects get delayed or take longer than anticipated. With HOAs, the process is more drawn out, as there are multiple levels and people involved. But at any point during a project, your manager should be able to tell you its status.

The warning sign is when projects appear to get dropped without cause. There is talk of the project, maybe even the start of action, and then it just stops.

When you ask about it, you get answers like, "It's being looked into." Or worse, management has no idea that work has stopped.

There are plenty of legitimate reasons why a project might be delayed or stopped: funding may dry up, unexpected problems can increase the scope of work, legal issues, weather problems, etc. But no matter what the cause, your management should be aware and able to explain the reasoning.

One association began a project of re-landscaping. It had been talked about for months, different bids were obtained, funding was in place, and a contractor was selected. Work was set to begin but never did. Just before they were ready to begin the project, they discovered a major defect with their property. Emergency repairs needed to be made immediately, and the funds earmarked for landscaping now had to be used for this unscheduled fix. The landscaping project was tabled indefinitely.

This wasn't the fault of the management, and in this case, the manager quickly notified the owners of the situation. If management doesn't appear to be aware of projects or doesn't follow through, that is when you should be concerned.

BILLS ARE NOT BEING PAID.

If a vendor completes a job, he or she should be paid fully and in a timely manner.

As a homeowner, this one is a little harder to detect. You aren't privy to the invoices, contracts, and schedule of payments, so when someone goes unpaid, you may not be aware. Sometimes, though, the vendor may bring it to your attention. He or she may make a comment in passing to see if you can get the message to the right person.

Take a look around your community. Do you see a decline in services? Maybe the pool isn't being cleaned, or trash is not being picked up. Services that you expect are not being done. This is an indication that people aren't getting paid.

An extreme example of this was one HOA that held its meetings in the clubhouse. One month, we all began to gather for the meeting. As the call to order time got closer, the room got darker. A member flipped the light switch and nothing happened. It quickly became clear that there was no electricity. Turns out management never paid the bill.

If a worker brings to your attention that he or she hasn't been paid, take this matter to your board of directors immediately. This can be a serious issue that can be costly to the HOA, as vendors will suspend or discontinue services until payment is received.

VENDORS AND OUTSIDE SOURCES ARE COMPLAINING, OR WORSE, LEAVING.

Just as vendors disappearing was a warning of a bad board, this is also a red flag for management. If someone is willing to walk away from a paycheck, there is something wrong. Most vendors who work with HOAs understand the pay structure and the standard delays in getting paid.

When I submit an invoice to an HOA, I can expect payment anywhere from a few days to a few weeks. It's not unusual for me to submit an invoice at one board meeting and not get paid until the following meeting. That's normal, and I know that. But longer than thirty days and I start sending a reminder. If an invoice is outstanding after sixty days, I remove the account from the calendar.

If vendors—gardeners, pest control, security—you normally see start disappearing without apparent warning, try to find out why. This may be an indication of trouble. It doesn't necessarily mean management is to blame, because there could be other underlying reasons. But if you notice a mass exodus of service providers, along with some of the other warning signs, it can be that management isn't processing payments quickly, not responding to the vendors, or not providing correct information. All of these would be reasons for the HOA to take action with management.

One homeowner did just that when a guard who worked at his community for a long time told him that he was planning on leaving. The guard explained that he wasn't getting paid on a regular basis. The homeowner went to the board, and management was confronted. It turned out that the security company wasn't submitting its invoices. In fact, it hadn't supplied an invoice in over four months. The vendor was instructed to clean up its accounting practices, and management was asked to alert the board if something like this happened with this or any other vendor. It was the homeowner's decision to alert the board that brought the matter to light. Without his action, it would have gone unnoticed and the HOA would have lost good workers.

Handling Issues with Management

You may have picked up that each one of these signs has a caveat. It can be a sign that management isn't doing its job, but there also can be a good reason why the task didn't get accomplished.

I've said it before and I'll say it again: property managers work hard. They get demands thrown at them from all different sources, and most of them are skilled at handling that. So one or two of the above issues from time to time isn't a problem. But when the issues become routine or excessive, that's when it's time to be alarmed.

What happens if you are experiencing a number of these issues with your management? As a homeowner, your first step is to bring your concerns to the board's attention. This can be done in open forum or discussed privately with a board member.

Once the board is aware of the problems, it has the task of finding out if the complaints are legitimate. The board may have more information than you on why something did or didn't happen.

At one open forum, homeowners complained to the board about not getting follow-up phone calls. The board listened to the homeowners but didn't take any action with management because it knew what was transpiring. Another homeowner had filed a large lawsuit against the HOA and was bombarding both management and the board with demands. Every available second was going towards putting out this fire. The homeowners were right—their needs weren't being met—but the board was aware of the reasoning for this and knew that management wasn't to blame. The board also knew it was a temporary situation and explained that to the homeowners.

Even if your complaints are accurate, that isn't a reason to act drastically. Changing management isn't easy for an HOA, and it can bring everything to a standstill. Switching companies shouldn't be entered into quickly or lightly. Before making the leap, talk to both the manager and the higher-ups in the company.

The manager may simply not be aware that what he or she is doing isn't working. Once the manager knows about your concerns, he or she and the office can take steps to correct the problem. If homeowners feel they are being neglected, then an assistant may be added to facilitate communication. New policies and procedures can be implemented to suit the needs of your homeowners.

As a homeowner, be sure to utilize the resources available to you. If you can't reach your manager, ask to speak to someone else. If your HOA has online services to report problems and update homeowners, be sure to use them. If there are reasons you can't, then let the manager know.

If a manager just isn't working out—and it happens—the board can request a new manager. There may be another person within the company that is more suited to your needs. Of course, as a homeowner, you don't have the power to do this, but you can mention it to your board. Present your case clearly and calmly. Provide the board with examples. This is where the log I mentioned earlier could come in handy.

As a homeowner, you shouldn't be afraid to question management. Sometimes there's a reasonable explanation for what you think is a problem. Your attitude may change a bit once you are aware of it.

At one open forum, a homeowner came with a whole list of items that he thought the property manager failed to address during the month. The owner read his list off one by one, and then the manager responded to each point. The homeowner thought nothing had been done, but in reality, most of the issues had been addressed.

Sometimes, if things don't improve, a change in management companies is inevitable. At least if you have to go this route, then you know you gave it a fair shake. Now you can move on to finding a new, more suitable management team.

When you do make the switch, use your experiences with the prior company to evaluate the candidates for the position. Changing management companies may not be the easiest task your association faces, but it can be done professionally and smoothly. Sometimes a fresh start is just what everyone needs.

Contacting Management

As I've said, the management company is the liaison between you and your association. If you want to contact a board member, you go through management. If you need architectural approval, you go through management. If you need a repair, you go through management. If you need information about your HOA, you go through management. Just about anything you need from your HOA requires you to contact management.

Contacting the manager sounds like it should be an easy task. You call him up, tell him what you need, and you're done. In theory, it works beautifully, but in real life, communicating with management is one of the biggest sources of frustration for owners.

Now before I get a whole slew of managers angry at me, let me say that this isn't because the managers aren't doing their jobs. A lot of times, it's simply logistics. You work full-time, so it may not always be convenient to reach the management during business hours. Yet they are a business and only work during business hours. See the flaw?

Managers are also very busy. In vaudeville days, there was an act that involved spinning plates on tall poles. The performer would get one plate spinning at the tippy-top of a long stick, then start another one, then another, then he'd run back and spin the first few so the plates didn't fall. He would keep going until there were six or seven poles with plates twirling on the top, all at the same time. This is a good depiction of what a property manager does every day. He tries to keep the plates spinning without any breakage.

Just because your manager has a lot to juggle doesn't mean your needs should be forgotten. But it may help your cause to be patient, considerate, and a little bit accommodating.

When you need something, you want it done not only in a timely fashion but also correctly. That's not unreasonable. One way to accomplish this is to figure out the best way to contact your manager. Your manager may ask that you email her, or she may prefer phone calls. Others will ask that you contact their assistant. Each manager has a different style and preference, so find out which one works best for your manager and use it.

Provide your manager with the most efficient way to contact you, too. You'd be amazed how many people will ask that they receive a follow-up phone call but don't leave their number. They will assume management has it, but that's not always the case. At a meeting, one homeowner asked me to call her regarding a certain issue. I asked for her phone number three times and even gave her a piece of paper to write it down. She wrote her name and nothing else. At the next meeting, she complained that I never called her. I explained that she never gave me her number. She responded, "You could have found it."

You want your interactions with management to be as effortless as possible. Here are some ways to make the process transpire smoothly for both you and management.

HAVE WHAT'S NEEDED.

Have everything you need so management can fast-track your request. Sometimes a homeowner will need certain information from the HOA for his or her insurance, accountant, or architect. The homeowner will tell management to email the needed documents directly to his or her vendor. The manager will agree and ask for the address. The homeowner will say, "Oh, I don't have it; I'll have to get back to you." Be ready with all the information.

When it comes to filling out a form, follow the instructions. The reasoning may not be clear to you, but there may be an underlying reason why the specified requirements are there. Some HOAs require three sets of plans for architectural submittals. This may not seem reasonable to you, but the HOA has a reason for doing this—one is given to the architect, one is kept in your homeowner file, and one is returned to you stamped with approval. Not following the instructions can result in your request being rejected or delayed.

In order to expedite matters every time you contact your property manager, you should have the following information readily available:

- **Your name.** Sounds simple, but when we are worked up, we sometimes forget to state this basic info.
- **Property address.** This is the address you are calling about. If you are an off-site owner, your residential address may be different, but your manager needs the address of the property in the association.
- **Name of the HOA.** Often this is needed in order to get the proper information for you. Many people don't know the names of the HOAs they live in. A management company may have hundreds of properties and thousands of homeowners. To look each one up individually would take a lot of time.
- **Account.** This makes it easier for whoever answers the phone to locate you. Most accounts are coded by HOA and address, so giving this number allows the person on the other end to know exactly who you are and the property you are referencing.
- **Return phone number or contact information.** If you want or need management to respond to you, include that information. Having it readily available takes away the excuse of not being able to locate it.

Any time you contact management, whether it's through the phone, email, letter, or even in person, have this information ready to share. I recommend that you have it stored in your phone and computer so that you can just call it up. If you are sending a letter or email, you can copy and paste it into the body of the communication. If you are on the phone, it's all right there and you don't have to look anything up.

CONTACT THE CORRECT DEPARTMENT OR PERSON.

If you have an issue with your bill, talk to the accounting department. If you need documents for a real estate deal, talk to escrow. Find out who the right person is and deal directly with him or her. Deciphering who exactly the right person is may take a little bit of effort. Ask questions, find what department can best handle your needs, and get the name of the person whom you should deal with.

When you get ahold of someone who is extremely helpful, write down his or her name. The next time you have a concern, start with this contact. The contact may not be able to help you with this matter, but he or she might be able to point you in the right direction. It doesn't hurt to use whatever resources you have available to you.

ALLOW TIME.

Just the other day, I had a case come up with one association whose violations I handle. A member of the rules committee emailed me regarding a unit that had an infraction. He sent me an email asking how he should handle the situation. At that time, I was in the midst of an emergency situation for another HOA. When I was finally able to respond to his email, later that same day, he had already taken the matter into his own hands. Unfortunately, his remedy went against prior directives of the board and legal counsel and caused a delay in correcting the situation. It also resulted in additional work hours for me and the attorney.

Give management a chance to act. We live in an instantaneous society. We want things and we want them now. Unfortunately, HOAs haven't entered that world just yet. HOAs have channels and layers they have to go through, and sometimes that takes time. Be sure to allow adequate time for action.

There is nothing wrong with asking your manager when you can expect a response or action. Then if you haven't heard back, reach out again.

BE POLITE.

My mother always says, "You can catch more flies with honey than vinegar." Of course, my smart-aleck answer is always, "Why would I want a bunch of flies?", but her point is well taken. Generally, when you contact management, you need something. Right or wrong, people are more responsive to someone who is nice to them.

You demand respect from your manager, as is expected, but you also need to give it. At times you may get frustrated, and that's understandable. We all lose our cool every once in a while. But don't start out with an attitude.

REQUEST A FOLLOW-UP PHONE CALL OR NOTICE.

Often managers will get a message from a homeowner, take the action that is needed, and then move on to the next problem or issue. They assume you will assume that the task has been completed. That's a lot of assuming going on, so when you make the request, ask the manager to notify you when action is taken.

Allow the manager to choose whichever method—email or phone—works best for him.

If you notified management of a broken sprinkler, the manager may send you an email saying, "The landscapers have been notified and will be out this afternoon to make the repair." Then he or she will close the book on the matter. You may be expecting a call back when the repair is actually made and get frustrated when you don't receive it. The manager, on the other hand, assumes the gardener has made the fix and all is well. The manager has now moved on to the next crisis and doesn't realize you are waiting for a follow-up call. Let him or her know when you make the initial call that you would like to be notified when the work has been completed. Or you can take the lead and simply say, "I will call you next week to make sure this has been completed."

Some management companies also have online access for homeowners, in which you can check the status of any work order issued, whether for the community or your individual unit. The vendors and staff update the open requests as work is completed. If your HOA has this feature, it's beneficial to utilize it. It's designed to keep you informed in the quickest manner while allowing management to continue to work on other issues.

Remember that management is there to work for you, but sometimes you have to assist it in helping you. The goal is to get the desired action in the quickest and most efficient manner. This may mean taking the initiative and then allowing management to do its job.

PART FOUR

DISPUTES

Neighbor-to-Neighbor Disputes

You've probably heard the saying that "fences make good neighbors." Sometimes those fences are just not high enough or strong enough. The sides battle, and no slumpstone, wood, vinyl, or wrought-iron boundary is going to stop them. In some cases, you watch the conflict brew slowly. It starts with animosity that just grows and grows until it eventually erupts. It can get very sad, because you are also witnessing the destruction of a long-time friendship.

A neighbor-to-neighbor dispute is exactly what it sounds like. It is a disagreement or parting of the ways between homes, units, or parcels. As an example, maybe one neighbor has a pool in his backyard. It begins to leak, and the next thing you know, his neighbor's yard is flooded. The property owner who was flooded feels her neighbor should have known his pool had a problem and addressed it. The pool owner didn't know anything was wrong and feels that his neighbor should have said something if she thought something was amiss. This is a prime example of a neighbor-to-neighbor dispute. The HOA wouldn't be involved in this issue because the two properties butt up against each other and there's no HOA property involved. None of the association's rules were broken, and the two parties need to work it out for themselves.

Of course, often that is easier said than done.

Settling Neighbor-to-Neighbor Disputes

Just because you are neighbors doesn't mean you have to be friends. It's wonderful when that happens, but it's not always the case. You are purchasing a house, not the people who surround it. But you do have to live with those people, so you have to find a way to get along.

If you find yourself in a neighbor-to-neighbor dispute, there are steps you can take to remedy the situation. To begin with, assess what the real problem is, because it's hard to resolve a problem that you haven't admitted is there. You may be fighting over noise issues, but maybe the trouble really started when your neighbor began parking his car in front of your house. Figuring out the exact issue is the first step towards correcting it.

Once you know what the problem is, try talking to your neighbor. I do have to qualify this and offer a word of caution: don't put yourself in a dangerous situation. If for any reason you feel your person or personal property is at risk, skip this step. Safety comes first, and no one should be placed in a vulnerable or unsafe position.

In any other case, simply talking honestly and courteously to your neighbor is sometimes enough to remedy the situation. There are times, though, when the neighbor just doesn't care. His or her attitude is: "Big deal if I park in front of your house. Get over it."

It's at this point that you may want to reach out to your HOA. Explain the situation to the board. The board will review the situation and determine if any HOA rules have been broken. If there is a violation, the HOA can address that issue and may be able to bring up the other concerns you have with the owner.

It's important to note that once a violation is issued, the association can't share the details of what action is being taken or your neighbor's response. The most the association can tell you is that it is addressing the issue. Some homeowners feel that if they issued the complaint, they should be included on all the interaction. But homeowners do have a right to privacy, and just as you wouldn't want your information shared with others, the HOA can't share others' information with you.

Using IDR

What happens if the HOA determines that no rules are being broken? Does this mean you are completely on your own? Not necessarily.

Typically, if the dispute doesn't involve the HOA, you will be notified that it's not an HOA matter and you will need to handle it amongst yourselves. At this point, you can come before the board and request its assistance in the form of IDR.

IDR stands for Internal Dispute Resolution. Every association has a policy for this dispute mechanism. If it doesn't, then the policy established in Civil Code prevails. IDR is exactly what it sounds like. It is a chance for two sides to get together and discuss their differences in the hope of finding a solution. In a neighbor-to-neighbor situation, the association acts as the buffer.

The good thing about IDR is that it offers a neutral forum to talk. Sometimes these feuds escalate because we don't adequately communicate with one another. In a case involving two neighbors, it may also help to have a third party there. It's a bit harder to be petty or vindictive when someone else is present. Voicing opinions to a third, unbiased person can also help demonstrate the unreasonableness of an argument. It's like group therapy for community living.

If you think IDR would help your situation, you will need to request this measure in writing. To request, simply notify the association *in writing* that you would like to have an IDR and list the specific homeowner or owners. The notification details and structure for the actual IDR varies from HOA to HOA, so be sure to check your Year-End Disclosure packet for the correct process for your particular HOA. If you don't have it, you can request it from your management company.

Once the request is received, the association will contact the other party with the invitation to participate. A homeowner can refuse the invite. He or she doesn't have to sit down and meet with you. But if the homeowner agrees to the session, then management will coordinate with the parties and the board to find a mutually-agreed-upon date and time. The meeting will be scheduled at a neutral location, and the association will appoint at least one person to attend the IDR, usually a board member. Other board members may attend, but a quorum of the board is not necessary in order to hold the session.

At the IDR, both sides will be given an opportunity to speak. They can ask questions and voice concerns. The same rules of conduct that apply for any other meeting also apply to these sessions: be courteous, wait to be called on before speaking, and listen when others are talking. The facilitator will also be given an opportunity to speak. This person or persons may make some recommendations or suggestions to resolve the conflict.

Any agreement reached at the meeting will be finalized in writing and sent to both homeowners. An IDR may not be legally binding, but if a party goes against the mutually agreed solution, this can be used against him or her in any legal action.

To give you an idea of how the process works, here is a synopsis of one IDR I was involved in. It was a disagreement between two condo units, one on top of the other, and a very large dog. The owners in the upstairs unit allowed their hundred-pound dog to have free roam of the apartment. The unit below didn't mind, except at night. For some reason, Fido loved to run at one o'clock in the morning, creating a loud thumping noise in the unit below.

The downstairs couple went to the couple upstairs and asked them to please confine their dog at night. The dog owners were offended. They had no intention of confining their dog. And why should they? The couple downstairs made noise too.

This went on for weeks. The downstairs owners grew more and more frustrated, and the upstairs unit got angrier and angrier. Both sides threatened to sue each other and the HOA—they always threaten to sue the HOA.

Even though this was a neighbor-to-neighbor issue, IDR was recommended, and both sides accepted.

The parties showed up at the scheduled meeting. The downstairs owners stated their case by saying that the dog was large, and when it ran, the sound carried into their unit. They were willing to put up with it during the day, but at night, it was unacceptable. The upstairs neighbors countered that the couple below was just being unreasonable. The dog ran at night to get to their daughter, who had special needs. They couldn't believe their neighbors were forcing them to get rid of their dog.

The couple admitted that the husband had made that statement—that the upstairs neighbors needed to get rid of the dog—one day while in a fit of anger, but he hadn't really meant it. The couple said it was a sweet dog but just loud at night. And they didn't want the little girl to give up her pet. The downstairs couple now understood why their neighbors were so upset.

The husband and wife upstairs conceded that the dog could be loud, especially at night, and it was agreed that they would confine the dog in their daughter's bedroom at night and not allow him to roam the house.

Problem solved. The outcome was typed up and sent to both homeowners, and there weren't any more problems.

That's how the process should work, but it doesn't always go so smoothly. You may have a homeowner who refuses to participate or one who just won't make any concessions.

Some people will counter with the question of why they should go through the motions of requesting an IDR if their neighbor can simply refuse. The HOA can't force someone to agree to IDR, but if you are having an issue, it is a good method to try even if it's not successful.

One reason is that it shows you are being reasonable. If the case escalates, this will be a point in your favor. Courts look at what efforts the parties made to resolve the squabble. If you were willing to participate in IDR but the other side refused, it paints you in a better light. The court may also ask your neighbor for a reason for declining, and "I didn't want to" isn't the best answer to hand to a judge.

One association had an ongoing noise issue between neighbors. One woman sent in weekly complaints about the ruckus coming from her neighbor's unit. She complained of being unable to sleep and being forced out of her unit. She usually ended her complaint with "and the other residents are going to complain too." But they never did, and it was her word against the neighbor's.

The board recommended IDR. The noisy neighbor readily agreed as long as she wouldn't have to face the woman alone. The woman who complained about the noise adamantly refused. She wasn't going to take time out of her schedule to do this. She was informed that without the IDR, the association couldn't assist her in this neighbor-to-neighbor issue. Without any collaborating evidence or complaints from other units, it was just a matter of she said/she said. Moving forward, this person would have to file a noise compliant with the police department, as there was nothing else the HOA could do.

I should mention another avenue available to associations to handle disputes— and that is ADR, or Alternative Dispute Resolution. This is similar to IDR, but while IDR is handled all in-house, ADR involves a neutral third-party facilitator. ADR is the precursor to filing a legal claim, and in some incidents, an association must offer ADR before it can proceed with legal action. When faced with ADR—whether initiated by the association or a homeowner—most HOAs will seek legal advice on how best to handle the situation.

Don't be afraid or embarrassed to go to your association with a neighbor-to-neighbor dispute. I can guarantee you they've seen it all. From noise complaints, to leaks, to reckless driving, to parking, to planting a tree the neighbor doesn't like. The association's IDR is a mechanism that is available to you and should be used. I bet if the Hatfields and McCoys lived in an HOA, their whole little squabble would have been resolved with just one IDR session. (OK, maybe not, but that doesn't mean it won't work for you.) It's worth the effort.

Board Disputes

Wouldn't it be great if all boards got along? I know this may sound crazy, but my answer is no.

The best thing about having a governing body that makes decisions is that you get more than one opinion. Each member of the board brings his or her own perspective, his or her own questions, his or her own reasoning, and his or her own individual approach to problems. And you get to benefit from each and every one of them.

One board had a very strong president. She was decisive and intimidating. I was hired to work for her association because no one else would. In fact, I was paid more to take on this account. For some reason, I got along well with this woman and worked for her association for many years. But with all due respect, she was the judge, jury, and executioner for this HOA. What she said went.

Oh sure, there were other board members—four of them, to be precise. One didn't bother to show up, one would bring his dinner and eat during the meeting, and the other two would sit and chat while the meeting was going on. If a decision was needed, she would simply say, "We're all in favor, right?" and they would all nod in agreement. No one challenged what was voted on or asked questions. It was just done.

You may think this is an ideal way to run an HOA (no hassles and no conflict), but it isn't. And it wasn't in this case, either. The board—a.k.a. the president—ended up making a decision that got the association sued. And of course, when the going got tough, this fearless leader left. She resigned from the board, sold her unit, and moved on. The homeowners who allowed her to control their association were left to pick up the pieces when they lost the lawsuit.

It would be easy to just blame this president, but the rest of the board and the community have to be held accountable. The other board members were willing to allow the president to do their jobs, and the homeowners were content to leave things as status quo for years. No one wanted to step up, and members were content to let this one person do the work and dictate the running of the HOA.

You can also have the polar opposite of this board: the board that can't seem to agree on anything. The difference between this kind of board and the one above is that at least with the board that agrees on everything, things get done. When the board is in complete disagreement, nothing gets accomplished.

This happened with one board that faced some very challenging times because of its inability to get along. There were seven directors, and they were in constant conflict. Three would be on one side, and three would be on the other. No matter what issue came before the board, the outcome was 3–3 with the president as the deciding vote. This was the case for major decisions like approving contracts as well as minor ones like approving past minutes. One side voted aye, and the other was nay.

The president tried to be neutral and uninfluenced by either side. He would weigh the options and come to a conclusion. After one especially bad meeting of being pulled in two directions by each side, he asked me for a piece of paper and there on the spot wrote out his resignation. He was done. It was completely understandable, but it left the association in quite a pickle. With the board evenly split, they couldn't agree on a seventh member. Every vote was even-Steven, and no work could be conducted. The stalemate lasted for months.

It became even more ironic because both sides hired an attorney. Now we had not only a dueling board but also dueling legal counsel. I would love to tell you that everything turned out well with this association, but unfortunately the turmoil is still going on. Eventually, it will be resolved, but until then, the HOA has to suffer through it.

Disputes within the Board

Most boards find themselves somewhere in the middle. They generally agree, but every once in a while, they have their disagreements. Although meetings can get heated and uncomfortable when boards are in dispute, I feel this is the best scenario for the homeowners.

Why do I feel this way? When you have a board that isn't afraid to discuss issues and air differences, you usually end up with the best resolutions. Every time a decision is made, you can be comfortable that all sides have been looked at—the pros, the cons, the ups, and the downs. The outcome isn't rubberstamped. It has thought behind it. Even if you don't like the final decision, you can respect that the board went through a proper and thorough process.

There are going to be fights any time you have a gathering of people. If you don't believe me, just think back to when your relatives gather for Thanksgiving. These are people you know and love, and there is a whole pile of delicious food, and yet a topic inevitably comes up that gets everyone riled. But by the time you get to the pumpkin pie, all is forgotten and you move on to telling old family stories.

This was true even for a small condominium building I worked for that only had five units. Every unit had a seat on the board. I thought this account would be easy-peasy with only five members, but boy, was I wrong. Size really doesn't matter, even when dealing with an HOA board of directors.

The problem with board disputes is that they usually unfold publicly. Have you ever gone out to dinner with another couple and it's apparent that they have had a spat? No matter what you do, the tension and awkwardness are still there. That's how it is when your board is feuding. It makes for very long and tense meetings.

It would be fine if the discord affected only the board members involved, but the fallout from board fights can affect your whole association. If the board is spending its time at the meetings sniping at each other, then it isn't addressing business. If the turmoil continues, maintenance may begin to decline, approval for projects can be delayed, and a feeling of negativity can quickly spread through the community.

The trick with board disputes is to not let them affect the atmosphere of the community and its ability to get work done. In order to do this, board members must be willing to respect the other members' opinions.

If you, as a homeowner, find your board is ineffective due to disputes among itself, try to gather a group of homeowners to mediate the situation. Don't embarrass, reprimand, or take sides. Simply remind the board members that they do have a fiduciary responsibility and bickering doesn't accomplish that. Point out how it is affecting the homeowners individually and the overall community.

Sometimes all it takes for a board to correct its behavior is calling it out, so that the individuals can overcome their differences and move on.

If not, then as homeowners, you may have to take more drastic measures. The easiest of these would be to wait until the next election and vote the board out. Of course, in order to do this, you need other members who are willing to serve.

I've seen many homeowners complain about the way the board is acting, its inability to get tasks accomplished, and its lack of dedication to the job. At the board meetings, the members are saying, "It's time for a change." Yet when it's time for the election, the only ones with their names on the ballot are the board members. This is a sign that things aren't so bad. Otherwise, someone would step up to the plate.

The other option is to recall the board. This is a more drastic approach and is harder to accomplish. We talked about the process earlier in the chpater "Good Board, Bad Board." It is a measure that is available, but it shouldn't be entered into lightly. But know that if things with your board get unbearable, your community does have options.

Disputes between You and the Board

What happens if your board gets along just fine but there is a problem between you and the board? As a homeowner, this can be frustrating because you have no power. The board is the decision-making body, and you have to abide by its decisions.

These kinds of disputes tend to arise over violations, architectural approval, or some kind of project that you think should have been done but wasn't or was done and you think it shouldn't have been. Generally, it boils down to a difference of opinion. You want things one way, and the board thinks it should be another.

The good news is that this is usually the easiest kind of board dispute to remedy. It is, so to speak, a one-on-one fight.

If you find yourself in this kind of predicament, the first thing to do is approach it in a logical manner. Go to the board meeting and request the rationale for the board's decision. Don't be confrontational, but rather act as if you are on a fact-finding mission. You want to get as much information as you can.

You may be surprised to find out that the board agrees with you but has its hands tied by forces beyond its control. Then present the board with an appeal. In the appeal, you will ask the board to reconsider its previous decisions and give the reasons why you think it should honor your request.

Let's say you live in a condo and want to upgrade your windows. You put in the necessary paperwork, and the board denies your request. You go to the meeting and ask the board for its reasoning. They say, "The windows you want to install aren't consistent with others in the community." This may be a true statement, but that doesn't mean you don't have any recourse. Once you have the reason, you can now gather information. Find other examples of inconsistent windows in the community, if there are any. Find out if there is a way to change the community standards. Contact the manufacturer for any assistance they can offer. Some HOAs have requirements that are outdated, and the window-maker may be able to provide some stats that will sway the board.

Submit your findings in a written appeal and ask the board to reconsider them. Be willing to answer any questions that the board or management may have.

If the board refuses to look at your appeal or denies it again, you can request an IDR. Just like you can request an IDR with another homeowner, you can request this option with your board. The HOA cannot refuse a request for IDR, so the board will be required to meet and discuss the issue with you.

Remain professional during the IDR, no matter how tough that may be. Don't argue, yell, or belittle. It may make you feel better, but it's not productive. Instead, ask the board for a viable solution. They may have a remedy that you were unaware of.

Going back to the window analogy, one HOA had a homeowner who desperately wanted new windows. The association required that the color of the outside framing be almond. This wasn't a color that was normally stocked and was a specialty order, which of course made the price go way up. It made the project too rich for her blood. She went through the proper channels but was denied at each step. At IDR, she expressed her frustration, as she needed the windows to reduce noise. The board came up with a list of options to take to her vendor. One solution was to paint the frames, which the vendor said he could do but would void the warranty. That became a non-option. Another one was to somehow cover the frames in the right color. The vendor took this and came up with strips that could be epoxied to the frames. This didn't void the warranty for some reason, it gave the consistency the board wanted, and the homeowner got her new windows. Everyone was happy . . . especially the vendor, who ended up getting a lot of referrals for his HOA-compliant windows.

When it comes to working with your board, you have to keep in mind the adage "if at first you don't succeed, try, try again." You may need to be tireless to get what you want. You also have to be willing to compromise. You may not always get your way, the exact way you want, but you may come close.

Board disputes are a part of HOA living. Sometimes they will involve you, and other times you'll just be a spectator. In either case, the real issue comes down to how the parties involved handle the situation.

Management Disputes

Disagreements with your management company are a little harder to resolve. Unlike disputes with your neighbors and board, there isn't a formal process for addressing this kind of conflict. That doesn't mean, though, that you don't have options for handling conflicts with management.

Generally, disputes with management have to do with procedures that aren't being followed by one side or the other. It's usually compounded by the perception of a lack of respect.

For example, as a homeowner, you may have an issue that needs attention. You go through the proper channels, and nothing seems to be getting done. Your frustrations mount because you feel management is being dismissive. In this situation, it doesn't really matter who is in the right because it doesn't change the way you feel, and homeowners should never be made to feel like they don't matter.

Settling Management Disputes

If you find yourself in a head-to-head battle with your management, the first thing you should do is speak to *your* manager—not his assistant, not even his superior, but the person who is in charge of your account. This should be done even if this is the person whom you have the issue with.

Again, in a calm and rational manner, present your case. Explain your opinion and why you feel you don't deserve to be treated this way. Allow the manager to express his or her side. Listen to what he or she has to say. Sometimes the frustration we experience is due to not wanting to hear what we are being told. It's not that we're not getting the information; it's that we don't like the information we're given. No one likes to be told "no," but sometimes that happens and we get upset with the person who is telling it to us.

After trying this, if you still aren't getting the result you expect or just getting a whole bunch of attitude, then it's time to speak to a supervisor or the person above your manager. The same steps apply here. Explain your case in a calm and rational manner. Avoid name-calling or badmouthing anyone else. Just stick to the facts. Continue up the chain of command if you have to. Find someone who will listen and who will take the action you need.

The person you deal with at the management company doesn't have to be your manager or a supervisor. It can be the receptionist, another manager, or anyone who you find to be helpful.

One homeowner called me because she needed information regarding her property. She was frustrated because she wasn't getting what she needed. I asked her what steps she had taken. She said she had called and left messages. She said, "If I call back again, Claire is going to get mad." Claire was the receptionist. I asked her if she had asked Claire for help. She hadn't thought of that. Within an hour, she phoned back to tell me Claire had been able to assist her.

Befriending Claire was a good idea because even if she didn't have the needed information, she had access to the people who did. Use whatever sources you have available.

If you still feel like you aren't getting anywhere, the next step would be to address your concerns with your board of directors. The board hires the management, and it should be made aware if you are being treated unfairly. The board also carries some clout and may be able to get things done for you.

This can be a bit tricky, because to contact the board, you have to go through management. It's a little tough to say, "I don't think you're doing your job, so can you let the people who hired you know that?" If you are uncomfortable going through the management chain of command, then broach the topic at a board meeting. Ask the board if you may address them in executive session. Once you are in executive session, you can request that management be asked to step out of the room. This will allow you to air your concerns without having to face your manager directly.

The board does have the right to refuse your request to have management leave, and the manager will remain. Don't let that sway you from your mission. State your case clearly, as if the manager weren't there.

Some people are afraid to square off with their manager, so they drop the issue instead of facing the manager. In my history, most managers will volunteer to leave to allow you to discuss your issues with the board privately.

Whether you choose to address the board with or without management present, you should have some examples to back up your complaints. This will help the board when they tackle your concerns with the management company. It will also guide the board in determining if this is an isolated incident or if it is more rampant.

There is no guarantee that the board will take any action on your claims, but you do get the satisfaction of getting them off your chest. That may not be the best solution and probably not the one you wanted, but it does help a tiny bit. Also, management will now be aware that the board is on alert, and it may spring them into action. The end result is to get things accomplished, and just knowing the board is aware may be the catalyst management needs to take your matter seriously.

If problems persist between you and the manager, you may need to take action to protect yourself, legally. One step would be to communicate with your manager solely in writing. Emails are a great way to protect yourself. It creates a paper trail that you can maintain. The manager may say, "She never notified us of that," whatever "that" may be. If it is in writing, you have the proof that you did. You'll also have the manager's responses, and the dates, times, and names of the people you contacted. Now no one can claim that they weren't contacted. Having everything documented will allow the board to see if management has been doing the job or just giving lip service.

Sometimes there are reasons for delays or what appears to be inaction, and having the paper trail can help determine the cause of a problem. Recently, one homeowner was having an issue with a repair in her unit. She was furious that the HOA's contractor wasn't showing up. Work wasn't getting done, and her unit was in disarray. She went to the board to demand something be done, as the project was going on way too long. The manager was able to produce the email trail. There were emails from him to the contractor and to the tenant confirming the date for the work. Then there were emails from the contractor stating the tenant wouldn't allow access to the unit. The last batch was the manager reaching out to the tenant only to be told, "It's not a good day for me; I have to take my mother to the doctor's."

In this case, it wasn't the manager's fault at all, but the paper trail allowed the homeowner to see exactly where the problem rested. She talked with her tenants and immediately had the unit available for the needed work.

In another incident, a manager was having trouble with a homeowner, and the board thought it might be useful if I got involved to help resolve the matter. The homeowner ended up pitting me and the manager against each other. She would tell me that the manager had told her that what she was doing was OK, and she would tell him the same thing about me. We knew what she was doing and went to the board with our recommendation: approve a policy that any communication with this one owner had to be in writing. This way, everything was spelled out. She couldn't say I told her she could break the rules, because it would be in writing that I told her the opposite. It worked. It protected me, the manager, and the association. When the homeowner found her tactics weren't working, she moved on.

You can use the same technique. Put all your requests in writing. Your first written request should be to the manager, with a copy to the board stating that until further notice, all communication with you from the association will need to be in writing. The board and management should honor this request because it protects them as well.

Of course, you have to abide by it too. Even though it's more effort, be sure to document all activity with management in writing. This doesn't mean you can't call, but follow that phone conversation with an email. Something like, "I just left you a message to find out when my unit will be inspected for termites. Please let me know the date. Thank you."

Even in a dispute, remain courteous, even though it can be trying at times. And yes, the same goes for the management company. They should be treating you in the same manner no matter what the situation.

Using IDR

Just as with the neighbor-to-neighbor and board disputes, if you aren't getting any satisfaction, you can request IDR. The IDR would be with the board and not the management company, because the manager is an agent of the association. This means he or she is acting on the behalf and at the direction of the board. If there is a problem, it is up to the board to remedy it. And that is why the IDR would be with them.

Even though the IDR is very similar to discussing the issue with the board, it is a bit more formal. If the matter proceeds to legal action, having the IDR can be beneficial. I recommend that you avoid legal action when possible, but if you are forced down that road, you want to make sure you've taken the correct steps along the way. There's nothing more exasperating than standing in front of a judge and hearing the other side say, "We wanted to work it out, but she refused."

We're going to do an about-face right now. So far, we've been talking about the negative aspects of management, but let's give them some credit where credit is due. I don't think anyone aspires to be a property manager. It is a job that was created out of necessity, and people tend to fall into it.

Being a property manager is not an easy job. You are working for a lot of different people with their unique personalities. So acknowledge those managers when they do a great job. Maybe you had a situation come up and the manager stepped up to the plate for you. Just as you would file a grievance with the manager's supervisor and the board for a wrongdoing, you should make them aware when the manager goes the extra mile for you. It will be appreciated. And going that extra step to recognize a good deed may help you when you need assistance in the future.

At times it may be hard to believe, but you and your manager are on the same team. You have the same objectives—you want the community to thrive and to live in peace. Work together, and you can accomplish those goals.

Legal Disputes

It would be great if you could read this book and all your disagreements would magically disappear. I once worked with a board member who, on his candidate nomination form when running for the board, put down that his goal for the community was "to sing songs and eat marshmallows." It was his humorous way of saying it would be nice if everyone got along. It's a nice thought but unfortunately unrealistic. In fact, his response generated some harsh feedback from other homeowners who felt he wasn't taking the matter seriously.

Disagreements do come up. Battles erupt. And people just don't see eye-to-eye. Sometimes it's the HOA's fault; other times it's the homeowner's. And then there's another scenario where it's neither the HOA nor the homeowner's fault, but rather a third party's.

Let's look at a little scenario. A man—we'll call him Chas—decides to rob a house owned by Bob and Nellie. He surveys the property and determines that the side steps are the best point of entry, as they are out of sight. He waits until after dark and then begins his plan to break in to the house. As he is trying to gain entry, he falls through the side steps. The noise alerts Bob, who calls the police.

The police come and end up taking Chas to the hospital, as he was injured in the fall. Chas immediately files a lawsuit against Bob and Nellie. He maintains that the steps were deteriorating, and the couple failed to maintain their property, therefore putting him in danger.

Bob and Nellie counter with the argument that the steps were never used, and therefore there was no reason to maintain them. Guests at their property came in through either the front or back doors. Besides, they had potted plants in front of the steps to discourage someone from using them. Most importantly, though, Chas wasn't invited onto the property and therefore was trespassing and assumed any liability.

So who wins?

Answer: the lawyers.

I bring up this story not to demonstrate that lawyers are evil and should be avoided but rather to show that there are always at least two sides to every lawsuit and possibly more, depending on the number of litigants. I've worked for hundreds of HOAs, and not one has gone unscathed when it comes to legal issues. I don't know of one HOA that hasn't been sued or had to file a lawsuit against someone. Lawsuits can be the biggest sucker of energy, resources, and money for an association. For those reasons, I recommend that you avoid them if possible.

Before we go any further, I think it's important to stress that lawyers are not the piranhas they are sometimes made out to be. I've worked with legal counsel for many homeowner associations. For the most part, these men and women are ethical, are hardworking, and want to settle disputes as quickly and painlessly as possible. They don't spearhead a fight, but they also don't back down when attacked.

Earlier, I said that lawsuits should be avoided *if possible*. I was going to say *at all costs*, but that just isn't right. Unfortunately, there are times when no matter how hard you try, you simply can't resolve an issue. Either it is too important to drop or one side just isn't willing to let the issue go. Sometimes the only solution is to litigate, but that should be a last resort, not the first.

Avoiding a Lawsuit

I remember when I was in my twenties and had an opportunity to buy a business. I had reached a deal with the selling party, and then everything stalled. The negotiations started getting hinky, and my attorney advised walking away. I was outraged. I had negotiated in good faith, and I felt like the business owners should keep their end of the bargain. My attorney said, "You can go to court and force them to sell you the business. They can tie it up for years and, in the meantime, run the business into the ground. You'll be spending a lot of money for a business that won't be worth a dime." He was right. The prize wasn't going to be worth the fight. He gave me some additional advice: "Always try to avoid legal action. Once you get into a courtroom, you never know what the outcome is going to be."

It was good advice. I've seen it happen many times while working with HOAs. An owner or board files a lawsuit that is a "sure thing." Everyone agrees, except the judge, who rules otherwise. I've seen HOAs that thought they couldn't lose end up having to pay millions of dollars and homeowners who thought they would make a killing walk away with nothing but a bunch of attorney fees.

Here are some steps you can take to avoid a lawsuit.

COMMUNICATE.

So how do you avoid a lawsuit without giving up your rights or principles? The first step—whether it's with an HOA, a neighbor, or a business or it's a personal issue—is to communicate. Talk to the powers that be. Sometimes legal action can be avoided simply by opening the channels of communication.

BE FLEXIBLE.

Here in California, we get Santa Ana winds. They are strong, hot winds that blow through at high and consistent speeds. In Los Angeles, we also have incredible and tall palm trees. You see these tall, straight, sturdy trees and wonder how they can survive the harsh Santa Anas. The reason they do is that they bend.

Sometimes in legal actions, you have to be like those palm trees. You have to sway a little this way and sometimes that way. If the trees were rigid, they would break as soon as the winds hit. If you stand firm and are unrelenting, you may actually be doing yourself more harm than good.

PUT HARD FEELINGS ASIDE.

We tend to be very protective when it comes to our homes and our families, as well we should. Any time someone goes after our home, our first inclination is to fight. But sometimes the best thing we can do for our families and ourselves is to walk away. We may not have been treated fairly or ethically, but it's not worth destroying what we do have. Lawsuits are time consuming and can be expensive. It's not worth winning the battle to ultimately lose the war.

HAVE A SOLUTION.

With that said, always have a solution or a resolution that you would be willing to accept. It may be a certain monetary amount or an action that needs to be taken. Have something in mind that you would find acceptable and be willing to negotiate towards.

Often, when legal settlements are being formatted, you will be asked to decide on an amount that you are authorized to accept. You don't tell the other side what this amount is. If they come in higher, great—you take it and run. If they don't meet your limit, you tell them to go back and sharpen their pencils. But having a predetermined limit allows you to accept a settlement on the spot.

There is an old anecdote that says you can tell a judge has made the right decision when neither side is happy. This is especially true with HOAs. Don't expect to get everything you ask for, because it normally doesn't happen.

ASK FOR WHAT'S FAIR.

Many people, even some who live in your own community, view HOAs as deep pockets. They have money, so why shouldn't you get a little piece of the pie? This can turn something that should be a quick and easy fix into a large legal battle.

Imagine you got into a little fender-bender. You tapped the car in front of you and damaged the bumper. You follow all the rules of the road: exchange information, contact the police, take pictures, and notify your insurance. It's not that big of a deal. It probably will cost you a few hundred bucks. Then you hear from your insurance company that the other party wants $1,000. Sounds like a lot, but not worth fighting over. You agree to pay this amount just to put this behind you only to find out that the other driver declined your offer and is suing you for $84,000. You have no choice now but to fight.

That may sound extreme, but it happens quite a bit with associations. People believe the HOA or its insurance will just pay, and that's not the case.

KNOW WHEN TO WALK AWAY.

It's not fair, but sometimes you have to cut your losses. Legal avenues aren't cheap. The costs for a lawsuit can quickly start to add up, and pretty soon you could be facing thousands of dollars in legal fees. You may be in the right, but is it worth spending $25,000 in the hopes of winning $10,000? Sometimes the best way to win a lawsuit is to never enter into it to begin with.

Homeowner Legal Disputes

As a homeowner, filing a lawsuit shouldn't be a knee-jerk reaction or a method for getting the board to do something you want.

For example, a homeowner may want to paint his house purple even though this is specifically against the rules. The homeowner may state or send a letter that says, "If you don't allow me to do this, I will have no option but to contact my attorney and file suit." Usually it's an empty threat.

It may be a hollow threat, but it is one that may force some associations to turn the matter over to their attorneys. Once this happens, the issue becomes more expensive, not only for the association but also for the homeowner, who now may have to hire his or her own attorney to answer the HOA's attorney. It's a vicious and often unnecessary cycle.

Homeowners should also be aware that when they sue their HOA, they are suing themselves. You are a member of that HOA and are a party to any decision or repercussions stemming from your lawsuit.

One association was sued by a member for an infraction of the architectural guidelines. He had completed an alteration to his home that the HOA said needed to be removed. He removed the work but then sued the HOA for the cost of removing the structure and restoring his property because he felt it was outside the association's scope. A court agreed with him and awarded him the sum of money he was seeking. The HOA immediately assessed all its homeowners to cover the legal fees and payout. Each member had to pay $1,100, including the homeowner who sued. When he didn't pay the amount, the association filed a lien. The homeowner went back to court and argued that he shouldn't have to pay the amount because the money was just going to him anyway. He lost this case and had to pay not only the judgment amount but also all the collection costs incurred by the HOA.

As a homeowner, there may be a time when legal action is the only option you have, and at that point, you should pursue it to the fullest. But legal action should be a last resort and not entered into lightly.

Association Legal Disputes

Associations shouldn't go looking for lawsuits either, but every association should be prepared to face one at some point in its existence. We live in a litigious society, and lawsuits are always a threat.

It is easy for an association to think, "We won't file a lawsuit," but you have no control over someone filing a lawsuit against the HOA. Often people see an HOA as easy money.

One year during the holidays, a homeowner in a very wealthy community had a family party. During the festivities, his sprinklers came on. When his guests were leaving, one gentleman slipped on the wet sidewalk. He was OK but within a few weeks filed a lawsuit against the homeowner (the host of the party and owner of the sprinklers) and the association (they owned the sidewalk). I think the theory behind this man's suit was that the homeowner (who was his relative) and the association would turn the matter over to their insurance and he would get a quick and easy check. No one would get hurt.

In a sense, an HOA is a deep pocket without a limit because it has the ability to special-assess homeowners for funds. If an association is sued, loses, and is unable to pay the judgment, then the homeowners or members are assessed. Each individual homeowner is now responsible for paying his or her fair share. If an HOA has 25 members, is sued for some reason, and loses or settles the case, the HOA or its insurance is responsible for the payout. Let's say the association's share of the awarded settlement is $50,000. If the HOA's insurance doesn't cover this and the association doesn't have enough in its accounts to pay this amount, it may be forced to pass an emergency special assessment. Each of the 25 homeowners would have to pay $2,000.00. All of a sudden, that faceless victim has a face.

Of course, the other argument is that that's what you pay insurance for. This is true, but insurance doesn't cover everything and also has limits. You may have experienced this with your own personal insurance. You go to the doctor's and expect the bill to be 100% covered, but a few weeks later, you get an invoice stating that there is "no coverage for this service." You are now responsible for the full amount.

This also happens with HOA insurance. Some items simply aren't covered, others are over the limit, and other times insurance will only cover part of the judgment or settlement. The members are now responsible for the remainder.

The worst case of this I ever saw was a lawsuit that was filed against an HOA by a contractor. The association lost to the tune of four million dollars. Each homeowner had to pay a sum of $30,000. The relationship between the two parties deteriorated so quickly that when the dust settled, homeowners had 30 days to pay their $30,000 share. Many homeowners were forced to declare bankruptcy.

Wondering what happened to our money-hungry cousin who slipped on the wet sidewalk from the story above? His family put pressure on him, and he withdrew his lawsuit. He probably is also spending holidays alone, as I'm not sure many members of his family want to risk inviting him over.

You'll often hear the board or management talk about liability, and people like him are the reason. Associations always have to be mindful of what could happen and the potential for a lawsuit. Unfortunately, this is the "sue-happy" society we now live in. We may have to accept it, but we don't have to become part of the problem.

Try to settle your disputes without involving the legal system. In the event you are forced to take legal action, you can be confident that you did everything you could to avoid that path.

Avoiding Disputes

A disagreement—whether it's with your neighbor, the board, management, or anyone else—is a source of stress and anxiety. The best way to eliminate this tension is to avoid it in the first place.

Of course, that's harder to do when you are the one affected by the situation. But if you find yourself involved in a disagreement with someone from your HOA, here are a few steps you may want to take.

COMMUNICATE.

Open the channels of communication. As you most likely can tell from the number of times I've mentioned it, communication is an important step. Don't ignore whatever the situation is or think it will just go away. It won't. Talk to your HOA and ask that it keep you informed.

Let's say you have a repair at your condo. The HOA is responsible and calls the plumber. You are told the plumber will be there Wednesday at 9:00 a.m., so you take the day off and wait. No plumber. At noon, you call the management company, only to find out that the work was rescheduled to Friday.

Now let's look at the same situation, only this time the plumber goes to your home and no one is there to let him or her in. The plumber hangs around for a bit but then has to move on. The manager reaches you, only to find out that you had an appointment scheduled and didn't want to miss it, so you left.

In the first scenario, management was wrong, and in the second, the fault lies with the homeowner. In either case, the conflict wouldn't have been an issue if the sides communicated with each other.

Communication is vital for any operation to run smoothly. And it goes both ways—the association needs to communicate with homeowners, and homeowners need to communicate with the association.

BE WILLING TO ASK FOR HELP.

Pride can be a wonderful thing, but it can also be the source of many disputes. We all need help sometimes, but you have to be able to ask for it. Homeowners who are having difficulties may need to reach out to their board and community. It's not easy but necessary.

After the Northridge earthquake, many homes sustained major damage. It took time, but most houses were eventually restored. There was one home in a community that wasn't making any effort to repair the damage. The board levied fine after fine after fine. There was no response from the homeowners. The windows on the home remained boarded up, debris was piled up in the driveway, and the property was an overall mess. The board filed a small claims action on the unpaid fines, but the homeowners never appeared in court, so the association won. The HOA was then able to foreclose on this house. The hope was to get someone in the house who would clean up and maintain the property. When the homeowner got the notice of foreclosure, she contacted the board and appeared at a hearing.

It was one of the saddest meetings I've ever attended. She explained that their home had sustained heavy damage in the earthquake, and they had no insurance coverage. She and her husband, who were both in their eighties, went out and hired a contractor. They paid the money upfront because he told them that was the protocol (it's not), and he promptly disappeared with their $50,000. They went to the police who filed a report but said the chances of recovering the money were slim. This was their life savings. As they were both in their eighties, they didn't have many options. The homeowner said they hadn't even told their children about their situation. The house was boarded up with no electricity and had been that way for almost two years. She said they always made excuses about why their family couldn't visit. She didn't know where they would go if they lost the house, as her husband had recently had a stroke.

The board could have easily said "too bad, so sad," but I'm happy to say this board was better than that. One board member asked her why she hadn't come to them sooner. She said they were embarrassed. I think most of us would be. The board jumped into action. One board member was a contractor and said he would stop by the next morning and see what needed to be done. He thought he might be able to find some vendors and suppliers who could help out. Another board member was in finances, and he set up an appointment to look into a reverse mortgage for the couple. They were able to stay in their home, and months later, she came back to the board to thank them for helping. Unfortunately, her husband had passed away, but she said one of his happiest moments was spending an afternoon with their grandson in their refurbished home.

That's an extreme case and one I hope never has to be repeated. This couple could have avoided a lot of heartache if they had just reached out. People are willing to help. All you have to do is give them a chance.

LOOK AT THE SITUATION FROM ALL SIDES.

As I said before, there are always two sides to every story, and sometimes there are more. Before a dispute escalates, stop and look at it from the other side. You don't have to agree with their opinion, but knowing why the other side is responding the way they are may help to reach a resolution.

One HOA learned the importance of this when a petition was initiated to open their pool twenty-four hours a day. The reasoning was that we live in California and it doesn't get all that cold and people have varying work hours. Why shouldn't someone who works late be able to come home and take a dip?

The opposing side was just as adamant. Even the board was split on the decision.

Both sides had valid reasons for their fight. When they finally got together and had a dialogue, both sides began to relent. The twenty-four-hour people realized that leaving it open all the time would put a burden on those homes by the pool and invite unnecessary visitors late at night. The other side saw that there were times when the hours could be easily extended. Eventually, a compromise was reached.

Whether we like it or not, not everyone shares our opinion. Accepting that fact and taking a little time to look at situations from the other side can help to eliminate animosity and lead to a smoother resolution.

GET THE FACTS.

Once they know the reason for the rules, most people will abide by them. If your

HOA doesn't provide you with the information you need, then seek it out. If you are being asked to observe a rule that you just don't think is fair, find out why the rule was put into place. Sometimes even your board won't know why.

Doing this research may not change your opinion, but it may give you more insight on how to approach the subject and more insight into why the rule is there. Once you have this information, a compromise may be easier to reach.

BE FLEXIBLE.

Every relationship is give and take, and that also goes for living in an HOA. The worst kind of conflict is where both sides are steadfast in their opinions. Neither side is going to give an inch. If neither side is willing to budge, all the mediation mechanisms in the world aren't going to matter. Be willing to give a bit.

Don't get me wrong—that doesn't mean you have to give in to whatever the other person says. You have the right to your opinion and to voice it, but be willing to accept a deal. Negotiating is a wonderful tool, and I'm in awe of people who possess this skill.

In the prior story about the pool hours, one side gave in to having the pool open at 6:00 a.m. five days a week in exchange for having it close at 9:00 p.m. five days a week.

BE TRUTHFUL.

Be honest with what your complaint is, and don't try to pad it. It may be tempting to boost your complaint, but if it's determined to be untrue, none of your concerns will be taken seriously. And make no mistake—the truth always seems to come out . . . one way or another.

One homeowner was having difficulty with his neighbor. His grievances were numerous. At one point, he reported his neighbor for a loud, boisterous party and smoking in the common area. He provided the dates of the party, sent pictures of the aftermath, and demanded action be taken. The association took action and notified the homeowner regarding the behavior of her tenants. The homeowner responded with the airline tickets, hotel receipts, and affidavit from her tenants saying that they were out of town on the date of the party. The homeowner who submitted the complaint admitted that he just assumed the nuisance was created by this unit and never really checked it out for himself. The outcome was that any future complaints from this homeowner had to be verified by another source. The HOA couldn't trust his reports on face value.

HAVE A SOLUTION.

Or better yet, solutions. Don't leave it up to the other side to dream up all the answers. Take some time and come up with a few of your own. Be sure the ideas you come up with are ones you can live with, because if the other side agrees, you can't go back and say, "No, wait, what I really want is this."

Before going into any IDR session or mediation, write down solutions you would be willing to accept. Think them through thoroughly and put them in a prioritized list. This list is for your benefit and doesn't need to be shared with anyone. It will help you go into the session prepared and with possible resolutions that you have thought through thoroughly.

One board president became skilled in doing just this when his HOA sued the developer. The development company was being sued by the HOA after completion of the project. After leaving the development, there were a few minor issues, but one major issue involved land owned by the HOA, which the HOA felt had been neglected by the developer, resulting in damage to the property. The board president was diligent in his pursuit of a settlement on the lawsuit. At every mediation, he had a list of all the scenarios that would be acceptable to the association. The first one was always take back the property. Everyone knew this was a long shot, but it didn't hurt to ask. This list wasn't something he divulged to the other side, but it was a cheat sheet so that if one idea failed, he had another one up his sleeve.

DON'T MAKE IT PERSONAL.

Although it's hard to believe, generally actions taken against you aren't personal. Oh sure, it may feel as if they are. That's normal. Someone is attacking your home, and in some cases, the way you live your life, but really they are asking you to abide by the terms you agreed to.

One homeowner was called to a hearing before the board for driving recklessly in the community. There were complaints and a video. When the homeowner appeared, she started by going after the board. She attacked the job they were doing, personal relationships with others in the community, and other violations that this homeowner felt weren't being handled. Nothing was off limits to her. The board listened to her tirade, and when it was over, the board president said, "We called you here to have a discussion, but you've turned this into a war."

Keep things on a business level. If someone tries to engage you in an unprofessional exchange, refuse to participate.

AVOID RETALIATION.

Vengeance may be sweet, but it's not smart. Sometimes things would have gone by the wayside if people had just been willing to walk away. Instead, one side files a complaint, then the other side hurls one back, then the first one throws another, and on and on like a tennis match. At some point, one or both sides gets tired of the volley and a battle ensues. This can get complicated, heated, and expensive. Stop before it goes that far.

TAKE A BREATH.

Breathe. Relax. Slow down. The momentum of an argument can push a dispute to new levels. We've all had fights where we lose control, and we either say or do something we regret. Before you get to that point, stop and take a big, deep breath. Calm yourself down so you don't say something in haste that ends up costing you.

I worked for a corporate executive, and that was his belief. In any fight, negotiations, or merger, he said the person who maintained his composure always got the best deal. You can lose your cool later, after the deal is signed. The same philosophy works with your HOA. Once you lose control, it's hard to recapture it. Stay calm and keep your composure.

FIGHT THE GOOD FIGHT.

Don't be afraid to fight for what you believe in. There is nothing wrong with battling for your beliefs. Most people will understand why you are pursuing your cause and will respect you for it. Just be sure the fight is fair.

Problems arise when the fight becomes dirty. I hate to admit it, but I've seen many unethical things during my tenure, and it never ceases to amaze me. Some people will do whatever it takes to get their way no matter who or what gets hurt. You know what is right and wrong, so stick to your morals. Don't fight dirty. You can end up losing much more than you ever thought possible.

Through the years, I've seen people resort to all kinds of tactics to win. These knock-down, drag-out fights can be not only financially draining for everyone involved but also emotionally. I've seen homeowners lose friendships, the respect of their colleagues, and even their health. One HOA was involved in a fight with a vendor. The vendor focused unfairly on an elderly couple in the complex during their lawsuit. The husband fought back. Eventually the HOA won, but the pressure got to this man and destroyed his health. He didn't live to share in the victory.

KNOW WHEN TO SURRENDER.

At some point, you will need to stop. No one can tell you what that point is, though. That is a decision you have to make. Whatever you are fighting for may be worth abandoning if your health is suffering, your family is in distress, or you are losing more than you will ever gain. But this is just an HOA, and chances are whatever you are fighting over isn't worth risking the things that are most important to you.

Be honest with yourself and listen to your loved ones. Don't be ashamed to walk away.

KEEP A SENSE OF HUMOR.

Never, never, never lose your sense of humor. It is the greatest tool you have in dealing not only with your HOA but with your life.

Unfortunately, disputes are a part of community living. There are people who don't believe the rules apply to them. You can't control how they behave, but you do have control over your conduct. When it comes to dealing with your HOA and neighbors, always try to be professional, courteous, and fair.

Frequently Asked Questions

Everyone feels their association is different, but the truth is they are more alike than you think. Sure, the names aren't the same and the styles of homes vary, but overall, they are made up of people. People with the same problems and concerns.

Here I'll answer some common questions I've heard in this industry.

Q: When I get the Rules and Regulations and CC&Rs in escrow, what should I look for?

A: Read the Rules thoroughly, keeping in mind your own lifestyle and what's important to you and your family. For example:

Children. Do you have kids who are going to want a swing set, a basketball stand, or to play in the streets? See if there are any restrictions on these or similar items. Some rules will prohibit playing ball in the common area or won't allow play structures that are visible from the street. If you are looking for a family-friendly home, make sure the rules don't discourage that.

Pets. Many HOAs have pet restrictions that may include weight limits, number of pets, and banning certain breeds. If you have a menagerie, you'll want to look for mentions of pets in both the Rules and Regs and the CC&Rs. For example, I am a fan of boxer dogs. I've had one almost all my life, but this is a breed of dog that is prohibited by some HOAs. If I were purchasing a home, this would be the first thing I would look for. I would want to make sure I could continue to own the dogs I love.

Work situation. If you are planning on running a business from your home, you will want to check what restrictions are in place. Some associations will allow it provided there is no foot traffic or signage. Others will limit the ways you can advertise. And there are some that will ban it completely.

Parking. Almost every community has restrictions on parking. You want to make sure the community you are moving into will be able to accommodate the number of cars you have, any recreational toys like jet skis or boats, and RVs. If these items are important to you, you want to figure out how you are going to handle the situation before you purchase the property.

Recreational hours. What times are the facilities going to be available to you? It doesn't help to be paying for an onsite gym if the only time it will be available to you is when you are at work. This also can be important if the home you are thinking of purchasing is in the vicinity of the recreational facilities. You may not want to purchase a home next to a pool that is open until midnight.

It's also a good idea to check out the other conditions of the amenities. One woman purchased a condo with a community pool. She thought this would be a great way to spend time with her three grandchildren. Soon after buying, she was informed that the rules limited her to only one guest at the pool. She wasn't able to use the pool with all of her grandkids.

Determine what issues are important to you, and review the governing documents with those specifics in mind.

Q: Why do I have to pay for amenities if I don't use them? I'm never at the pool, so why do I have to cover those expenses?

A: It would be virtually impossible for your association to operate as an à la carte menu. This means every homeowner would have to be assessed a different amount each month.

When you move into a community, you accept responsibility for your share of the common areas—all of the common areas. The association relies on that agreement to generate a budget and pay the bills. Not using an amenity can't be used to lower your dues.

Imagine how hard it would be to keep track of when and if a member used each one of the facilities. A homeowner used the pool last month, but not this month, so should a credit be issued for the month? What happens when winter hits and no one uses the pool? Who pays the bills then? This would be an administrative nightmare and impractical.

Q: If I'm in violation, why does the HOA have to send me a letter? Can't they just pick up the phone and call?

A: Although a friendly phone call may seem like the neighborly approach, there are reasons why this isn't practical.

From the managerial side, a phone call can turn a simple five-minute task into one that takes twenty minutes or more. I can draft, print, sign, and mail a violation letter in just a few minutes, and it's done. But phoning someone involves multiple steps. The first one is actually reaching that person. Making contact with an individual can take a few tries. When I do connect, the second step is explaining the condition that needs to be addressed. Sometimes the homeowner is understanding and agrees to remedy the problem immediately. That's the ideal outcome. Sometimes the homeowner gets angry and wants to fight the violation or argue with me. Usually this conversation goes something like, "Everyone else does it." Or, "Don't you have anything better to do with your time than bother me with petty violations?" Or the homeowner wants the person on the phone to change the rules or grant him or her a variance. This person doesn't have the authority to do so, and the homeowner must present his or her request to the board. Depending on how heated the conversation gets, this phone call can turn into a twenty-minute exchange or more.

A normal association can send out over twenty-five violation letters a month. Sending out these letters takes approximately two hours. The same task done by calling homeowners stretches into eight hours, and that's time that the manager could be spending doing other work for your HOA.

Even if the homeowner is cordial and doesn't have an issue with the violation notification, the conversation can still be stretched out. Why? It's not unusual for a homeowner to take advantage of the situation to inform the manager of things he or she has noticed or ask questions that he or she has, "since I have you on the phone." And there's nothing wrong with that. You're entitled to ask questions, but it does take time away from the management staff. When you multiply that time by the number of homeowners in your association, you can see how it may eat into the workday.

This topic recently came up at an open forum. A homeowner was incensed that he had been sent a violation letter. He couldn't believe the board had approved this nonsense, as it was such a waste of time. The ironic part was his speech to explain to the board that the association was wasting time took over eight minutes! And this was just a one-sided conversation.

As a homeowner, there is also one very good reason for wanting to receive the notice of violation in writing. It's one way to provide you with protection. Phone conversations can be misconstrued, misunderstood, or simply forgotten. What was actually said and the content of a conversation can be argued, but with a letter, everything is spelled out in black and white. It leaves little room for disagreements.

Q: Shouldn't a board be expected to get input from all the homeowners before making a decision?

A: Think back to the last time you went out to dinner with a group of friends. The conversation probably went something like this.

"Where do you want to go to dinner?"

"I don't know. Where do you want to go to dinner?"

"How about pizza?"

"I don't want pizza. Let's do Chinese?"

"Nah."

You get the idea. You banter back and forth, and nothing gets decided.

Now multiply that by the number of members in your association, and you'll see why this isn't practical. It's one of the reasons the HOA forefathers . . . whoever they were . . . implemented boards. The board represents you and votes on your behalf. Hopefully the elected board members do their due diligence, make informed decisions, and take action in the best interest of the association.

If board members have to consult with homeowners before making decisions, the process will be drawn out and the chances for discord will increase dramatically.

That doesn't mean that you can't give your opinion in open forum. In fact, that's part of the reason for the open forum: to allow homeowners to freely voice their viewpoints. The board doesn't have to take your recommendations, but it does have to listen.

In some cases, a board may decide to take a straw vote in the form of a survey. It isn't required to adhere to the outcome, but it can be an indication of how the community is thinking before the board jumps into a large project.

If the association is facing a large project—revising the rules, the streets, painting, remodeling the clubhouse—the board may also elect to form a committee and solicit homeowners to serve on the committee. This is one way for a board to get more input from its members.

There are certain times when a vote of the membership is mandated, like for an amendment to the CC&Rs, but for the everyday operations, your board uses its discretion.

Q: Isn't the board required to get three bids for all work?

A: There is no requirement for doing this unless your governing documents include this specification. Most boards have a policy of getting three bids or more for large expenditures. It is a good practice, and I am always amazed at how the bids can vary for the exact same scope of work.

Depending on the vendors and the work to be done, a lot of boards will throw out the top and the low bids and go with the middle proposal. The idea here is that a really high bidder probably doesn't want the job. The bidder will do it, but he or she is going to make sure it is worth his or her while, and that means you pay for it. The lowball bid may not be experienced enough to know what the job entails or uses the low estimate to get the job and will add in change orders during the project.

A good board, though, will evaluate each bid and the vendor and make a rational decision. For example, the high bid may have included items that weren't in the original scope of work but will be needed. When you weigh that in, the bid isn't so outlandish after all.

For everyday, run-of-the-mill tasks, you don't want to solicit three bids. Your association or management should have a team of vendors that they have previously vetted and worked with who can be asked to do the work. For example, let's say a truck backs into the wall at your entrance and breaks the stucco. The damage is minor, and the repair will only be a couple hundred dollars. To ask three vendors to come out and give their bids is a waste of their time and of management's, who may have to meet them at the site. It also takes time, as the contractors have to work it into their schedules. It's more efficient to call a vendor whom the association has worked with, say, "Give me a bid," and get the job done.

Associations that ask vendors for bids but continue to use the same standby people they've been relying on end up running out of vendors to choose from. Contractors will stop providing estimates or ask for a fee as they get leery of continuing to bid projects with no results.

Another consideration is that the board may have already researched vendors. Let's say there is a portion of the sidewalk in your community that is breaking up and needs to be replaced. Management calls out three different concrete vendors to look at and bid the project. The board reviews the proposals and selects one vendor to do the work. Two months after this job is completed, a different section of pavement has the same issue and needs to be replaced. The board has already investigated contractors. Instead of going through the exact same exercise, it just gets a bid from the prior contractor and proceeds with the repair.

For large-scale, extensive, expensive projects, it is always a good idea to get three or more qualified bids. This makes good sense for your HOA as well as for you, as an individual homeowner.

Q: Why does it take the association so long to get anything done?

A: This is the question I get asked the most, and it's a big source of frustration for homeowners.

If you decide to paint your house, you contact painters and get a couple of estimates. Let's say you decide to go with Joe's Painting. You call Joe and schedule the work. Joe begins painting. In a few days, he's done. You inspect the work, it looks nice, and you hand Joe a check. All done.

So why isn't this same process utilized by your HOA when doing work? The HOA has more levels to go through. When estimates are received, they are reviewed by the board. The board is the only body that can make the decision of which contract to sign, and it has to be discussed at a meeting. If the bids come in around the time of the meeting (most managers will request that the bids be submitted in time for the meeting), then the board can discuss and decide. If additional information is needed, then the manager has to go back to the vendor, and the process can be pushed back another thirty days. Even if the board agrees to hold a special meeting to vote on this matter, four days' notice is needed to hold the meeting. Depending on the proposal amount and the complexity, the contract may need to go to legal counsel for review. This can take a few days. If the lawyer has changes, then there can be back and forth between the two parties. Once an agreement is reached, the work can commence.

All of this takes time and, unfortunately, is done out of the sight of homeowners. To the homeowners, it looks as if nothing is getting done, but that's not the case. An HOA with a strong communication system can notify homeowners of the steps. If that kind of mechanism isn't in place, then usually the only way homeowners can find out the status of a project is either by going to a meeting or word of mouth.

Q: Why is it more expensive for my association to get work done? I can get the same work done on my home for a whole lot less.

A: Again, this is another question I hear quite a bit. And it is true—work at an association can be costlier than an individual hiring a contractor to do work.

Let's take the same example of Joe's Painting that we used above. You hire Joe, he does the work, you like it, and you hand him a check. It's a simple, easy process.

But now Joe is working for your HOA. Before he can begin the process, he has to provide proof that he is licensed, bonded, and insured. Most HOAs require this for any work done in the community that costs over $500. Insurance that covers HOAs can be costly, and that cost is passed on to the association.

When Joe paints your house, the only person he has to please is you, and your spouse, if you have one, but in an HOA, there are a whole bunch of people. There is the board that hired Joe, the manager who probably will be overseeing the job, and every single homeowner or resident who lives in the community.

And then, of course, you have the added challenge of dealing with possibly hundreds of extra-watchful eyes. Every homeowner has an opinion, and some are not afraid to express it.

One community has a homeowner who is notorious for stopping work in the community. No matter what is being done, he is an expert and steps in to make sure the work is being done correctly. In his opinion, it usually isn't, and he stops the work. Management has to come out to assess the situation and then convince the vendor to go back to work. Contractors know that this type of encounter is not uncommon (almost every HOA has a homeowner like this) and take that into consideration when they bid projects.

Everything progresses along, and Joe finishes the job. He now submits his invoice. This is given to management for payment. Management begins the process of cutting the check and forwarding it to the board for signature. (Some HOAs require two board member signatures, which can take an even longer time.) Only then is the check mailed to the vendor. This process can take anywhere from a week to six weeks. And that's if everything goes along smoothly. Any hiccups along the way, like homeowner complaints, work that needs to be inspected, or board members who are unavailable to check the completed work or sign a check, can cause an even longer delay.

Vendors who work with HOAs know these limitations and take all that into consideration when pricing a job. These are the small items that can cause the fees to jump.

Q: I want to file a complaint against my neighbor, but I'm afraid of retaliation. Can I file an anonymous complaint?

A: A board should never act on an anonymous complaint. There is no way for the board or management to know if the complaint is coming from a valid source or just someone who may have an axe to grind. If you do have a complaint, you must be willing to put your name on it.

Most boards have a policy of not releasing the names of the person or people who make a complaint. In some cases, it is obvious and you have to decide if you want to continue with the procedure. Sometimes homeowners will complain about another homeowner during the open forum of the meeting, but the minutes should not reflect either party's name or address. As a recording secretary, if I feel information presented at a meeting could cause any kind of future retaliation, I will omit it from the completed minutes.

If you want the HOA to pursue a complaint with a homeowner, you will need to submit a written, signed statement. One community has a resident who allows his dog to run free. He can be a little unreasonable when he gets angry, so homeowners are afraid to cross him. His neighbors have contacted me regarding it but added this little disclaimer: "John's dog was loose tonight, but you didn't hear it from me." There's nothing the HOA can do with that. Without a name attached to a complaint or independent verification (a board member or management witnessing the condition), it is just a rumor, and the HOA can't take action on rumors.

Most boards, though, will make every effort to hide your identity for as long as possible. One caveat with this is that if the matter escalates to legal action, the original complaint can be demanded, and you may be required to be a witness. This is not normal, as in most cases, the matter never gets that far. It is something you should be aware of if you plan to file a complaint with your HOA. The association can and usually will keep it confidential but can only do so up to a certain point.

Q: Are we the worst association you've ever had to deal with?

A: This is my absolute favorite question that I get asked. Almost every HOA asks it, and all but one is wrong. A mild disagreement may break out at a meeting, and afterwards, a homeowner will come up and say, "We probably are your worst association."

Trust me, I've seen a lot in working for homeowners associations. I am constantly amazed by people—sometimes in a good way, sometimes in a not-so-good way. But it is always interesting.

Every HOA has spats, and every HOA has a tough meeting now and again. It's OK. Keep in mind the goals you have for your community, and you'll do just fine.

And the worst association I've ever had? I won't give you the name, but I will tell you the moment it earned the title. The members fought constantly and meanly. During one month, the president of the association got sick. At the next meeting, they announced that he had passed away. The homeowners who were at the meeting . . . applauded.

Not a community I would ever want to live in, and one I no longer wanted to work for.

So every time you think you have it bad, just remember that story and realize you can survive whatever your HOA may be dealing with.

Conclusion

Although we've been discussing the trials and tribulations that may arise from living in an HOA, it doesn't have to be a source of stress. The two main skills needed to succeed with your HOA are at your fingertips—education and communication. Armed with the knowledge of how your association operates and the rights that every homeowner has, you can tackle most problems that may arise. Using effective communication skills can help eliminate the discord that can fester and grow into full-blown animosity and turmoil.

Bottom line, everyone—homeowners, your board, and management—is working towards the same goal—to make your community pleasant, desirable, and prosperous. With a little bit of respect, patience, and camaraderie, there is no reason why your home can't be your castle. And no reason you can't succeed with your homeowners association.

Enjoy it. You've worked hard for it.

About the Author

Linda Perret has worked for homeowners associations for twenty years. Using her skills as a writer, she has attended thousands of board meetings and supplied minutes to numerous HOAs. In doing this work, she learned about the business of running a homeowners association. She continues to work with management companies and HOAs on providing secretarial services and consulting.

Linda also is a comedy writer and has supplied funny material to a slew of performers including Terry Fator, Joan Rivers, and Bob Hope. She is currently collaborating with her father, Gene, on a collection of gift joke books for all occasions. The author has also launched a free joke service and can be contacted at www.jokecrafters.com.

ABOUT FAMILIUS

Welcome to a place where parents are celebrated, not compared. Where heart is at the center of our families, and family at the center of our homes. Where boo-boos are still kissed, cake beaters are still licked, and mistakes are still okay. Welcome to a place where books—and family— are beautiful. Familius: a book publisher dedicated to helping families be happy.

Visit Our Website: www.familius.com

Our website is a different kind of place. Get inspired, read articles, discover books, watch videos, connect with our family experts, download books and apps and audiobooks, and along the way, discover how values and happy family life go together.

Join Our Family

There are lots of ways to connect with us! Subscribe to our newsletters at www.familius.com to receive uplifting daily inspiration, essays from our Pater Familius, a free ebook every month, and the first word on special discounts and Familius news.

Become an Expert

Familius authors and other established writers interested in helping families be happy are invited to join our family and contribute online content. If you have something important to say on the family, join our expert community by applying at:

www.familius.com/apply-to-become-a-familius-expert

Get Bulk Discounts

If you feel a few friends and family might benefit from what you've read, let us know and we'll be happy to provide you with quantity discounts. Simply email us at orders@familius.com.

Website: www.familius.com

Facebook: www.facebook.com/paterfamilius

Twitter: @familiustalk, @paterfamilius1

Pinterest: www.pinterest.com/familius

The most important work you

ever do will be within the walls

of your own home.

CPSIA information can be obtained
at www.ICGtesting.com
Printed in the USA
FSOW01n1808210716
22955FS